# Common Good Nation

It is time to create a parallel nation based on agreement rather than geography

TERRY MOLLNER

The Love Skill Publishing

Published and distributed in the United States by THE LOVE SKILL Publishing
61 Baker Road, Shutesbury, MA 01072
www.eldering.today, www.theloveskill.com, www.commongoodcapitalism.org



Cover design and text and layout: Greg Caulton
Logo and infographic: Israel Santana

Printed by CreateSpace.com

Common Good Nation / Terry Mollner

ISBN-13: 978-1546430155
ISBN-10: 1546430156

Printed in the United States of America

Any views expressed in this book, *Common Good Nation,* are my own and do not necessarily reflect those of the Calvert Funds, Calvert Investment Management, Inc. or my fellow Trustees/Directors on the Calvert Funds Boards or Calvert Foundation; nor those of StakeHolders Capital, Inc.

$19.95 US

*For our human society*

# Contents

# Introduction

IT IS TIME TO CREATE A PARALLEL NATION DEFINED BY agreement rather than geography. It is also time to create a more mature form of democracy.

Currently we are all members of nations defined by the land each occupies. For instance, the United States is the land between Canada's land and Mexico's land.

It is 2017, not 1017. The Earth is now one village. It is time for like thinking people living in all nations to unite to create the lives they choose.

Currently and usually, they have to wait until all the people who live on a particular piece of land can reach a majority decision for something to happen. For instance, why should some of us have to wait until Paul Ryan and Donald Trump join us in a majority decision before we can do something we think is sensible? We can now create an organization based on a worldview, invite those who share it to join it, and in the private sector create the for-profit and non-profit organizations we choose.

*We can create a parallel nation of like thinking people.*

The Common Good Nation (CGN) proposed herein is not in conflict with the geographic nations. It will be loved by them. It will be the equivalent of a free research and development program. Anything we create in the private sector that works well will more easily gain widespread support throughout the geographic nations. It can implement a similar program or support the ones we create in the private sector with, for instance, tax incentives.

The CGN will only attend to things not being done well or at all by the geographically defined nations. It will also create programs that will help the geographically defined nations operate better. What is currently being done well enough will be left to the geographically defined nations, such as the placement of stop signs and providing sewage systems and electricity.

Secondly, our current democracies are an immature form of democracy. In practice, they tend to be the last form of dictatorship before true democracy, a dictatorship of the majority over the minority.

As defined herein, *a mature democracy* is primarily the result of periodic discussions without a deadline toward eventual near consensus on issues. The process is cooperative and a genuine search for truth. In the absence of a near consensus, agreements for action are as much as possible based on an honoring of the direction in which discussions suggest our thinking is heading.

For instance, there was a time when all thought the Earth is flat. Then some guessed it was round. Then more. Today nearly all agree the Earth is round because it is round. It took time for the vote to move toward a consensus agreement on the truth that it is round. It often takes time for an individual to mature in his or her thinking to find truth. It also takes time for the people in a community to mature in their thinking to find truth.

*The wonderful thing about truth is that once we know it we can't ever fool ourselves into thinking we do not know it.*

Once we know how to use chopsticks with one hand, we do not go back to using them with two hands. Once we know a more efficient and enjoyable route to the grocery store, we consistently use it. Thus, once truth is found in each situation all sustain their belief and agreement on what it is, just as we all now sustain our belief and agreement that the Earth is round.

In this book, two organizations will be suggested that will move us in the direction of a mature democracy: CGN and People's Committees. The CGN will be described and all who share its worldview will be invited to join it. The People's Committees will be a program launched by the CGN to assist the geographic nations in focusing on issues and the discovery of truth together.

*What unites the citizens of the CGN is a particular worldview.*

The best example of current organizations that behave as agreement nations, at least to a significant degree, are religious organizations. They are based on a worldview, have members in nearly all nations, and have agreements its "citizens" keep to remain members.

I was born and raised in the Catholic Church, in Saint Joseph's Parish in Omaha, Nebraska, USA. Our leadership was in the Vatican, also a geographic nation surrounded by Italy. To remain a Catholic I had to be baptized, go to Mass on Sundays, and believe that the Pope was infallible:

he has a direct relationship with God and when he speaks in official forms it is the truth received directly from God.

Think of an agreement nation as a non-profit membership organization with members able to reside anywhere on Earth. What makes it different from other non-profit organizations is that, like geographic nations, its highest priority is meeting all, not some, of the needs and wants of its citizens (its members).

*The CGN you will be invited to join is a mature democracy based on a particular worldview. If you share that worldview, you may be interested in joining it.*

For instance, the CGN described herein will focus on building strong local communities of friends and the eldering of our children to full maturity in the skill of self-consciousness before they leave home. It will set in motion a program that will eventually end poverty on Earth. It will form associations of businesses committed to a capitalism that gives priority to the common good and second priority to profit. And it will initiate organizations such as People's Committees to improve the performance of the geographic nations where our citizens live.

A People's Committee, the second main organization being proposed in this book, is a program able to exist both in the geographic nations and the CGN.

They facilitate periodic discussions on important issues with the goal of at least 70% support for a position on each issue. It will be more thoroughly described in *Chapter 7: Some of the Projects That Could Be Launched by the Common Good Nation/People's Committees: A Parallel Political System With No Legal Power, But the Greatest Political Power.* Here is a brief introduction of it. This description is of one created in a geographic nation.

For-profit and non-profit organizations throughout the community select their most mature statesperson to be their representative on the People's Committee. These representatives sits in a circle, there is a skilled facilitator, and the community members can sit around them or witness what is occurring on local television or cellphones or listen on the radio.

At each meeting an issue currently important to the community is discussed. As long as a resolution receives a 40% vote, another session is scheduled, which could be in a week, month, or next year. Meetings continue to be scheduled to discuss the issue until there is a 70% vote of support for a resolution that states its position on the issue.

*The People's Committee will have no legal power. However, it will have the greatest political power in the community.*

Usually, no one will be able to easily win an election if the candidate does not support the positions receiving 70% support of the People's Committee or is clearly heading in that direction, for instance with a 55%, 63%, or more support for a resolution.

To a great degree, the People's Committee program will escape all the marketing, fake news, trickery, and manipulation present in elections today. Also, instead of focusing on the horserace between candidates the focus is on issues and the building toward a consensus on each.

*Through a cooperative process, those who choose to be involved in a People's Committee will be participating in a genuine search for truth.*

It is through the formation of the CGN and People's Committees that we can in a loving way mature our majoritarian democracies into mature democracies.

# 1
# Common Good Nation

IT IS NOT 1776. IT IS 2017. SURELY IN 241 YEARS WE HAVE discovered a more mature way to do democracy.

Does it really make sense to have over 100 million people vote for one of two people for President? Only a few people know either one of them well and almost no one knows both of them well. This makes us vulnerable to smart marketing, trickery, and fake news. We also do not have in depth knowledge of their positions on major issues because discussions of them usually do not keep our attention focused on the television screen to watch the commercials. The media coverage becomes solely the horserace.

*Representatives of any group of people are best chosen by the people in the group, the people who know each other well. This is a direct and personal process and most free of the effects of marketing.*

Bringing about this change in our American election process will not happen soon or easily. However, creating the CGN can be very helpful as a demonstration of a more mature form of democracy.

The people living on any piece of land on Earth will have many different worldviews, basic beliefs about life. To ask them to reach a majority vote on anything is also not the best way to reach decisions, especially if the process is a competitive one where winning becomes more important than truth. The CGN will model a more mature form of democracy, one where leaders are elected in groups of a hundred or less where everyone knows everyone else well.

The geographic nations will love it. It will be the equivalent of a free research and development program. Anything the CGN comes up with that works well can then be supported by the geographic nations. With strong evidence of success, they could be launched in the geographic nation and easily embraced by all. Or the geographic nations can determine it is best to leave them in the private sector and provide support such as tax incentives.

The first thing that distinguishes the CGN from geographic nations is that it fully honors individual freedom—anyone can join or leave it at any time without having to move or deal with any of the other demands of a change of geographic nation. It is not easy to cease being an American and become a French or Japanese citizen.

*Thus, the CGN fully honors individual freedom whereas that is not easily a possibility for geographic nations. One can join or leave a CGN at any time*

Secondly, the most frustrating problem with the geographic nations is that the worldviews of the citizens are all over the map. To achieve a majority vote necessitates responding to many extreme positions or having the current majority determine the choice. For many possible reasons, those in the majority may be stuck in a very immature way of thinking.

These are the main two reasons people who share its worldview will join the CGN:

### *Two Main Reasons People Will Love the Common Good Nation*

1. it fully honors individual freedom, and
2. it is based on a more specific worldview they share.

A third reason many will embrace it is that, except for a small annual citizenship fee to know who is a member for the following year, it will not have taxation. Fees and donations will cover expenses.

A fourth reason is it will be loved by geographic nations. It will not be in conflict with them. It will only attend to things not being done well or at all by the geographic nations. It will also focus on programs that will make the geographic nations work better for their citizens. For example, it could develop People's Committees briefly described in the *Introduction.*

A fifth reason many will embrace the CGN is that it will use a more mature form of democracy. Instead of having 100 million people go to the polls to choose a President, only groups of people who know each other well will choose leaders.

For instance, the fundamental structure of the CGN is communities of friends. These will most often be freely chosen communities of friends. However, they could also be some of the members of congregations of churches, synagogues, and temples; areas of a town; local supporters of an even narrower philosophy; or any other way of forming a local community that share the CGN worldview.

Each Community would elect an Elder Body and a Community Board of Facilitators. It will also elect two representatives from its Elder Body to the Local Association's Elder Body, and two representatives from its Board of Facilitators to the Local Association's Congress. The Elder Body at that Local Association level would elect two representatives of it to the Second Association, for instance a Regional Association. The Local Congress would also elect two representatives to the Regional Association. This pattern would continue until all communities are represented by Associations that have less than 100 members in their Elder Body and Congress.

*In this way, only people who know each other well will be electing representatives to the next level bodies and no campaigns and political contributions will be necessary.*

There is much more to be said about this democratic model that will be described later. However, what is important to point out now is that the greatest power could always be at the most local level. It would first be with the individual, secondly with the Community, thirdly with the Local Association, fourthly with the Regional Association, and on up. Everyone is also free to participate or not participate in any program developed by their Community or any level of Association.

Secondly, the priority of an Elder Body is to make sure all decisions give priority to the common good. The priority of the Congress is to make sure there will be widespread support for any program they create to respond to the needs and wants expressed by the citizens.

Finally, the current democratic systems in our geographic nations can be easily gamed by self-interested parties, everything from getting control of state legislators by one political party so they can draw the federal Congressional lines such that a significant majority of their state's Congress people will always be representing their party at the federal level to fake news to marketing smarts and trickery. When people are only participating in electing people to lead them from within groups small enough where everyone knows everyone else, the choice is more grounded in reality with manipulation being much more difficult to accomplish. Also, in our modern Information Age it is possible to have all activities visible to all. Thus, all can now easily monitor on an on-going basis the performance of their representatives.

While fully loyal to both, their geographic nation and the CGN, people will slowly evolve into giving priority to the CGN and second priority to their geographic nation. Since people from all geographic nations can become members of the CGN, this could ultimately reduce the importance of the geographic nations and raise the importance of the CGN. Most wars begin between geographic nations. This would eventually, let's hope sooner than later, reduce this possibility and also the need for expenditures on armaments.

In summary, the main reasons people will eventually choose to be citizens of the Common Good Nation are the following:

### *Ten Reasons the Common Good Nation Will Emerge*

1. It fully honors individual freedom. It is possible for anyone on Earth to join or leave it at any time without having to physically move or deal with any other demands of switching geographic nations.
2. The agreement— the constitution—that unites them is based on a worldview they share. It is a nation of like-thinking people. This will make it easier to reach agreement on policies and programs.
3. It will not have taxation. Fees and donations will cover expenses.
4. It will not be in conflict with the geographic nations and even be fully embraced by them as a free research and development program.
5. It will use a more mature form of democracy where people only choose leaders from within a group where everyone knows everyone else well.
6. The ultimate power will be at the most local level, beginning with the individual, then his or her Community, then the Local Association, and on up. Thus, programs have to be attractive to members to be successful.
7. At every level, there is a check on the Congress by an Elder Body focused solely on making sure the highest priority, at all times and in all decisions, is the common good.

8. The Information Age allows all proceedings to be visible to everyone. This openness and transparency can serve as a second double check on the actions of representatives.
9. Ultimately, while being fully loyal to both, citizens will eventually give priority to the CGN over their geographic nations. This will reduce the importance of geographic nations as the fundamental structure of Earth. Since the CGN will have citizens in nearly all the geographic nations, this in turn can reduce the possibilities of geographic nation wars and the amount of capital spent on armaments.
10. The other side of the coin of giving priority to individual freedom is the making and keeping of agreements. In the CGN there will be a respected process for facilitating a resolution of differences through a cooperative search for truth rather than competition.

# 2
# Common Good Nation Constitution

IN THIS BOOK, I AM PROPOSING THE CREATION OF THE "Common Good Nation (CGN)," a nation defined by agreement rather than the land it occupies.

There will be some who will agree and some who will not agree with its worldview. That is as it should be. The purpose for creating the Common Good Nation is to have a narrower worldview as the unifying agreement so like-thinking people can more easily unite on the creation of programs its citizens will enthusiastically embrace.

*None of them have to participate in any program.*

That is one of the beauties of the CGN: the ultimate power is in the hands of the individual citizen. None of them have to participate in any of the programs that emerge. At the same time, by having a narrower common umbrella worldview, it will be easier to design programs that many will like and enthusiastically want to participate in as part of making the CGN successful.

*In the CGN, once agreements are made they are kept.*

Human life is agreements, with ourselves and others. The foundation of CGN is respect for both each person's ability and right to exercise individual free choice and the making and keeping of agreements.

*Agreements are seen as the other side of the coin of individual freedom of choice. They are an affirmation of the reality that we are all in this together.*

Allow me to present the proposed constitution for the CGN. The rational for some of the particulars in it will be explained in the next chapter, *Chapter 3: Why This Constitution at This Time.*

# Common Good Nation Constitution

## Preamble

We hold these truths to be self-evident in direct experience:

1. The universe is an indivisible whole. Coming to know this in direct experience and consistently living according to it is the foundation of full maturity in the human skill of self-consciousness.
2. The universe is going somewhere: it is maturing. We do not know the forms it will take years in the future; but we do know that, fundamentally, it is consistently maturing and currently mainly through us.
3. Since the universe is an indivisible whole, cooperation is the fundamental process in nature, and maturation is the particular kind of cooperation that is the fundamental process in nature. Cooperation is a process. It does not reveal the reason for the process. Maturation is the reason all the parts of the universe cooperate with each other. Competition is a lower form of cooperation, not possible without agreement that what is being competed over is important to both parties (the cooperative context). For human beings, compromise is a more mature form of cooperation, agreement is an even more mature form of cooperation, and love is the most mature form of cooperation (self-consciously together giving priority to participation in the maturation of the universe, the common good).
4. All things are conscious, that is, they are being one thing rather than another. Human beings can also be self-conscious. We can know what we are doing while we are doing it. We can analyze the past, plan for the future, and consistently execute the plan in the present. It includes being able to exercise free choice to continue doing what we are doing or switching to doing something else. Rather than only reacting, human beings can be watchers and choosers. We also change our self-definition as we mature up the layers of maturity of the skill of self-consciousness.

5. It is our human languages that allow us to be self-conscious. A human language is the creation of the illusion that the universe is an immense number of separate parts. This allows us to give each part a sound and symbol, called a "word." This allows us to talk about them with each other and ourselves. The universe is not separate parts. It is an indivisible whole. However, it is this mutually agreed upon illusion tool that it is separate parts, called "human languages," that allow us to be self-conscious.
6. The existence of human beings is a layer of maturity of the universe that allows it to be self-conscious in billions of locations at the same time. We are not born with the skill of self-consciousness. Like any skill, there are smaller skills where each one builds on the previous one with no smaller skill in the natural progression able to be skipped. When the highest smaller skill is mastered and all the smaller skills are integrated together into one skill and habit we have achieved mature self-consciousness. The human brain is not sufficiently developed to allow a human being to achieve full maturity in the skill of self-consciousness until the teen years. Then it is possible to master the remaining smaller skills to become fully mature in the skill of self-consciousness by the end of the teen years.
7. There are many models of the layers of maturity of the skill of self-consciousness. The following model is one of the many but it identifies the key maturation layers:

a. Baby—the priority is responding to sensations

b. Toddler—the priority is responding to differences, especially the fundamental feeling of happy-not happy.

c. Child—a human language has been learned and the priority is now getting what one's physical body wants within the illusion that the parts of the universe are separate from one another and we are each one of them.

d. Teen—the priority is one's ability and right of exercising individual freedom of choice.

e. Adult—one's most important free choice is discovered to be one's fundamental worldview that is now chosen and given priority. Life is now meaningful: there is a reason to do one thing rather than another.

f. Elder—the priority in the use of the skill of self-consciousness is the accurate fundamental worldview represented in words as, "The universe is an indivisible whole."

g. Mature Elder—the priority in the use of the skill of self-consciousness is the self-conscious experience of the oneness of nature, not the words representing it. This results in always giving priority to the self-conscious experience of oneness, second priority to relating with the parts of the universe where one's attention lies as inside and an extension of it, and third priority to the relationship action of eldering. Eldering comes naturally when full maturity in the skill of self-consciousness has been achieved. It is each moment giving priority with what is right in front of us to what we each decide is our best action for the maturation of the universe. Throughout history this has most often been labeled "moral behavior."

8. Contented happiness (often referred to as "enlightenment") is the result of achieving full maturity in the skill of self-consciousness. Each moment the only priority in action that sustains this experience is eldering.

9. The mastery of the skill of self-consciousness is the mastery of a human skill. We can each choose any religious, philosophical, scientific, or other belief to give priority above the mastery of this skill.

10. The mastery of the skill of self-consciousness is the mastery of the relationship among the oneness of nature; the mutually agreed upon illusion tool of separate parts that allow us to create human languages and become self-conscious; and our physical bodies that are the only part of the universe where, from the inside, we have sole and complete control.

**Articles**

*Article One:* Our highest priority as a nation is eldering ourselves, each other, and our children to full maturity in the skill of self-consciousness as early in life as possible. This is the only permanent way to end immature behavior by human beings.

*Article Two:* Anytime two people come together they often experience

# Common Good Nation

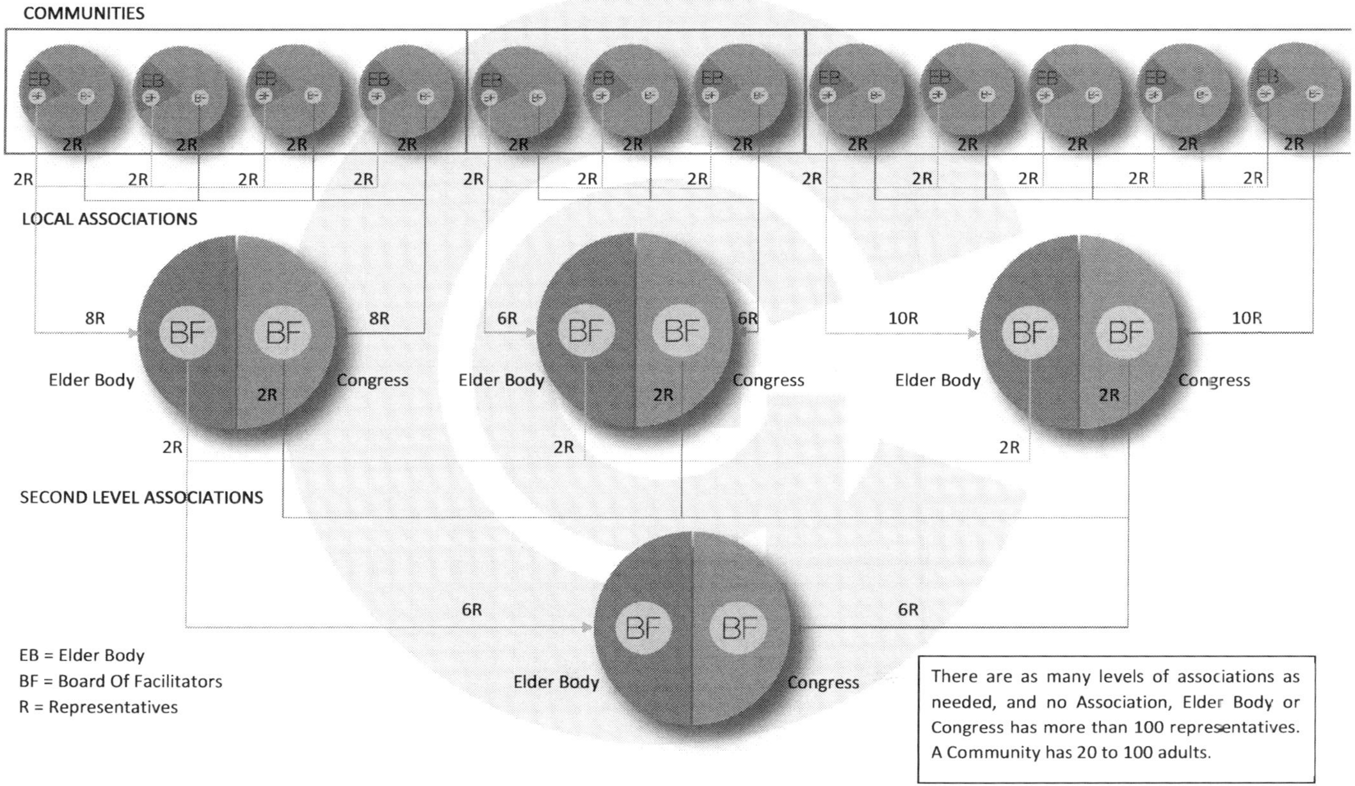

themselves as having two choices: to compete or cooperate. If they choose to compete, they are consistently in conflict. Not fun. If they choose to cooperate, they have used their human skill of self-consciousness to make an *agreement.* The agreement is to give priority to the two of them as if they are two parts of a whole. This can be great fun and result in a romantic relationship, friendship, or partnership. If many people choose to do this, we call it a "community" or "society." Anyone in a society who is not at all times giving priority to the common good of the society has left it and is now in competition with it. The only thing more important to give priority than the society is each person's direct self-conscious experience of oneness, the universe as a society. CGN honors the latter as each person's natural highest priority when full maturity in the skill of self-consciousness has been achieved. Since each person is accepting full responsibility to self-elder himself or herself to full maturity in the skill of self-consciousness and this is the highest priority of the CGN, it will usually be easy for all to agree on programs for the common good, programs that are direct participation in the maturation of the universe.

*Article Three:* In governance, each adult citizen (18 years of age) has one vote.

*Article Four:* Anyone who genuinely agrees with the worldview in the Preamble is invited to become a citizen of the CGN. Citizens can remain individual citizens, be members of a Clan, or form or join a Community.

Citizens are encouraged to form freely chosen Communities of friends. A Community can be any number of citizens between twenty and one hundred adults (defined as eighteen years old or older). Clans are any group of citizens of less than twenty people. Communities participate in the governance process of the CGN. Individual members and Clans do not.

This structure is chosen to encourage citizens to join with friends to create Communities. They are groups of friends who have stepped up to being organized as a Community. It can be a safe, enjoyable, and playful place to live and raise one's children. It is also best able to elder each other and the children to full maturity in the skill of self-consciousness, the children hopefully to full maturity before they leave home.

Each Community elects a Board of Facilitators of at least six and best of ten people. Each also chooses members to be on the Elder Body. It also elects at least six and best of ten people to be its Board of Facilitators.

Each Community's and Elder Body's Board of Facilitators elects two of its members to serve as its representatives on the Local Association Congress and Elder Body. Each of them elects two representatives to the next level of Association, the First Association, perhaps at the regional or state level. This process continues until there is an Association of all the Associations. Normally, no Association will be larger than 100 representatives with it able to grow to be 130 members before it breaks into two Associations. Also, each time a citizen is elected to a higher Association's Congress Body or Elder Body, he or she is replaced with another representative.

The normal maximum of 100 people in a Community, Congress, and Elder Body is chosen because at this number all can get to know each other well so when leaders are being chosen they are being chosen by people who know each other well.

*Article Five:* The greatest power is at the most local level, first the individual, next the chosen Community, next the Local Association, then the First Association of Associations, on up. The purpose of the Associations is to facilitate the operations and maturation of the citizenry. It is not to make decisions and enforce them on the citizens. The citizens are at all times free to participate or not in each program at any level at any time.

*Article Six:* The Elder Body of each Community or Association has one primary responsibility: to make sure the highest priority of all activities in the CGN is direct participation in the maturation of the universe. This includes making sure all parents are encouraged to elder their children very artfully up and into the skill of each smaller layer of maturity of the skill of self-consciousness and into full maturity in it before their twenties. This includes the eldering of all into full maturity in the skill of self-consciousness as early in their lives as possible.

The Elder Body members are consistently assisting each other in the maturation of their eldering skills. Once a citizen is chosen to be on the Community's Elder Body the person remains on it for life or until he or she resigns or chooses to leave as the result of a Clearing Process. Elders easily volunteer to leave when they judge it best for the maturation of us all. They also easily remain on it when they judge it is best for the maturation of us all.

If a Community determines that its Elder Body is not functioning well and they are unable to change the Elder Body with its cooperation, it can cease being a Community and reconstitute itself as a new Community and elect another Elder Body. This is the way the Community can protect itself from an Elder Body that it no longer respects.

*Article Seven:* The Community's and Congress's Board of Facilitators is responsible for facilitating and managing the affairs of the Community or Association. The highest Association is *primarily* responsible for managing the CGN's relationship with other people and organizations. However, all Communities and Associations will be very active in their communities and will speak for the CGN locally. Any CGN citizen or Community's, Congress's, or Elder Body's Board of Facilitators is free to initiate any project he, she, or it deems wise to initiate.

*Article Eight:* At each Community and Association level there is a contract between the Elder Body Board of Facilitators and the Community's or Congress's Board of Facilitators. It has three parts:

1. **The Elder Body's Board of Facilitators has the ultimate power.** Its Board of Facilitators is the legal board of directors or equivalent of the organization, in the CGN labeled "Board of Facilitators." The Elder Body's Board of Facilitators has the ultimate governance power in the Community or Association.
2. **It delegates full responsibility for managing the CGN to the Community's or Congress's Board of Facilitators but maintains the right to veto any of its decisions.**
3. **The Elder Body's Board of Facilitators tries to never exercise its veto power.** It has at least two members who sit as *ex-officio members* (without vote) the Community's or Congress's Board of Facilitators. If they judge that it is not clear that a decision is giving priority to the

maturation of the universe, they can request a meeting between the Community's or Congress's Board of Facilitators and Elder Body Board of Facilitators, or secondly if acceptable to both Bodies, three or more representatives from each, for the purpose of the Elder Body Board of Facilitators being satisfied that the highest priority is the maturation of the universe. If an agreement cannot be reached, the Elder Body's Board of Facilitators has the right to veto the proposal or unilaterally change it. In extreme cases, it can ask the Community's or Congress's Board of Facilitators to have a new Board of Facilitators elected. The Elder Body's Board of Facilitators second responsibility is to make sure all are eldered to full maturity in the skill of self-consciousness. If accomplished, this should make achieving agreement easier. If not, its first priority is to make sure as best it can that all agreements represent full maturity in this skill.

*Article Nine:* There are no competitive elections. Each body, where people know each other well, chooses its representative(s) to any other body, usually decisions by a Community, Elder Body, or Congress. The process is cooperative elections. This is where those seeking or asked to consider the position go to the center of the circle. This way all the people who could be best for the role are considered. Each can then take a turn speaking to explain why he or she would be best for the role and answer questions. Citizens are then free to also share why they support one or more of the candidates. On each vote of those in attendance with the right to vote, each stands behind the person they choose to support. This adds a very visible and emotional experience to the voting. After each vote the candidates are asked if any of them judge it is best to drop out of the process. In response to previous comments, each remaining candidate adds additional information as to why each thinks he or she is best for the role and answers questions. Citizens are then also invited to share why they support a candidate. The vote is again taken by having each person in attendance stand behind his or her chosen candidate. This process continues until only two candidates are left. At that point, the two are asked to sit facing each other in the center of the circle and have a discussion to see if the two of them can decide which of the two of them they think would be best. Regardless of what they decide there is one last vote of all in attendance with the right to vote standing behind the person they choose. It is this final vote that determines the selection. A two-thirds vote only determines the choice if the process does not get down to only one candidate left after a reasonable period of time. This two-thirds vote option is to be avoided rather than easily defaulted to.

*Article Ten:* All disputes between individuals or groups are resolved using the Clearing Process. This is where the parties in conflict agree on the choice of members of any Elder Body and others to sit with them and facilitate a resolution acceptable to both parties. There are four procedures: data, feelings, judgments, wants, requests, and resolution. By agreement between the two disputing parties, a facilitator of the meeting is chosen. The first section is the sharing of the data. This is the sharing of relevant information all would agree is accurate if they were watching a video of what is being reported. The parties in question take turns sharing their data relevant to this conflict. The second session is the sharing of feelings. Each of the parties involved share their feelings as a result of this situation. The third section is a sharing of judgments about the other's behavior and one's behavior as well. The fourth section is the sharing of wants. Each of the parties involved share their wants regarding this matter. The fifth section is requests. Each of the parties involved shares their requests of the others and themselves. The sixth session is resolution. In the context of the information shared and with the help of all present, the parties are facilitated into finding a resolution both parties can genuinely embrace. It is then written down and two people are chosen by the disputants to monitor their keeping of the agreements present in the resolution until completion.

The highest priority is what is best for our direct participation in the maturation of the universe. If agreement cannot be reached, the parties are encouraged to pursue resolution using the processes available to them in the geographic nation(s). Since most would like to avoid that route, citizens will usually fully commit to the Clearing Process in the hopes of resolving the disagreement there.

*Article Eleven:* For all Bodies, a majority of members being present, in person or by electronic communications, will constitute a quorum. All decisions will be made by consensus. If after a reasonable period of time this is not possible, the decision is postponed until the next meeting at least a week in the future. If consensus cannot be achieved at the next meeting at least a week away, the decision can be determined by a two-thirds vote. The only exception to this is if by a two-thirds vote at the first meeting it is agreed that time is of the essence and a decision needs to be made at that meeting. Then if consensus is not possible the decision can be made by a two-thirds vote at the first meeting. This latter process should only be defaulted to if absolutely necessary.

*Article Twelve:* Each Community, Elder Body and Congress will have a Board of Facilitators and Chair with terms lasting no longer than two years with no term limits. The Communities' and Congresses' Board of Facilitators will always remember that their priority is not to behave as a paternalistic system but to discover what is ready to emerge, identify it, and build a genuine consensus of support for it and/or a program to bring something about that speaks to it. The Elder Body will always remember that the only permanent way to end immature behavior by human beings is for each person to be eldered and supported at self-eldering himself or herself to full maturity in the skill of self-consciousness.

*Article Thirteen:* The records of all meetings will be recorded, kept, and made available to all using the Internet. At the same time and by the decision of a majority of those present and constituting a quorum, it is acceptable for any portion of a meeting's discussions to be kept private and not recorded. However, all decisions are recorded.

*Article Fourteen:* Any officers of a body may be financially compensated upon a decision using the process described in Article Eleven. However, such a decision must be decided at two consecutive meetings with those absent at the first meeting having ample time to learn of the decision before the second meeting which must be at least one week in the future. At the Community and each Association level, both the Elder Body's and Community's or Congress's Boards of Facilitators must agree on the compensation of any and all those compensated at an Annual Meeting by a two-thirds vote. Financial compensation shall be reasonable but error on the side of frugality rather than excess. Since CGN will never be in debt, if capital is not available to pay compensation, citizens will serve without compensation.

*Article Fifteen:* Assuming there is a quorum of a body, anyone can be removed from a position without cause using the voting process described in Article Eleven. There must first be a Clearing Process with all in the Body encouraged to attend and to which the person in question must attend. If upon reasonable efforts the person in question is not able to attend, a Clearing Process shall occur without him or her. At the next meeting, at least a week in the future so all can learn what occurred at the Clearing Process, if a consensus cannot be reach by a two-thirds vote of the Body constituting a quorum, the person is not removed from his or her position. The removal can be without cause because what is most important is that the Body have full confidence that the person in the position is the best person in that position for the CGN.

*Article Sixteen:* Any rights and responsibilities not explicitly stated in this Constitution remain with the individual citizens.

*Article Seventeen:* Any person upon reading this Constitution declares their commitment to honor and support its worldview stated in the Preamble and the agreements in these Articles shall be able to become a citizen of the CGN. Anyone can end his or her membership at any time. Only individual human beings may become voting members. As an expression of support for the CGN, people can become citizens without being members of a Community. However, all participation in governance begins with being a member of a Community.

If any three citizens are concerned that a person joining or who is a citizen is not sincere in his or her commitment but rather is seeking to take CGN in a different direction or be disruptive, they can request a Clearing Process before or after the person(s) becomes a citizen(s) of the CGN. At least ten citizens and three members of Elder Bodies must participate in it. If the consensus of those participating minus the person or persons being considered for citizenship is that his, her, or their priority is not a sincere commitment to the Constitution, he, she, or they can be denied citizenship. This can be appealed to any Elder Body. It can arrange for another Clearing Process which will be the final decision.

*Article Eighteen:* Any for-profit or non-profit organization, including partnerships, cooperatives, and other legally structured entities, can join the CGN as an organization member. Only individual human beings may vote. However, organizations of all kinds are invited to join as organizational members. Any and all of those participating in these organizations are also welcome to join as individual members and be able to vote. Within the CGN the organizational members are free to self-organize themselves in any way they choose as long as no Congress votes against it. The organizational members are encouraged to participate in the ways they choose in support of the mission of the CGN.

*Article Nineteen:* There will be a small membership fee, not to exceed $50 in 2017 US Dollars, mainly for the purpose of making sure each citizen is committed to continuing to be a citizen. This must be received before the first of each year for a person to be a citizen with voting rights for the coming calendar year. A paper or electronic receipt from the Community for the membership fee must be sent and it is the citizen's evidence of being a citizen. The citizen's Community is responsible for the use of this money.

*Article Twenty:* Where it is legally possible, the CGN can issue a currency or currency equivalent. It can also issue an honest currency equivalent. This is where for every debit there is an equal credit and no one can create credits or debits outside of this process. This could be accomplished by using a bond fund, such as the Calvert Unrestricted Bond Fund. It is free to invest in any bond of any duration anywhere in the world. If a credit card and checking account service is provided, and the fund managers earn more than that necessary to cover the costs and rate of inflation in a particular country, using that nation's legal currency this can serve as an honest currency equivalent.

A digital currency could also be created. It could also be an honest currency with the capital being managed in the same way as above. Digital currencies could be created where the value of the currency would fluctuate. Through the use of a blockchain these currencies would be free of control by any party. It could also serve as an "equity equivalent." The capital could be used in a way that increases the value of this digital currency thereby being an investment option.

*Article Twenty-One:* One of the highest priorities of the CGN is to end poverty on Earth. If we now think of Earth as one village, this is one of the highest priorities of all the people in the village. CGN will support Trusts for All Children, Inc. (TAC) and/or similar programs that are dedicated to this purpose. TAC has two programs.

The first is called the "Common Good Fund." Donations are solicited for it. The capital is invested in common good corporations and investments. These are organizations committed to giving priority to the common good and second priority to profit or anything else. The annual profits, if any, are annually distributed directly to poor people to keep them above poverty. If possible, no administrative or other expenses are deducted from these profits. Every penny of profit is distributed to poor people. Warren Buffet and Bill and Melinda Gates have created an association of billionaires, now 115 members, who have all committed to donating 50% of their assets to charity before they die. The hope is that some of this capital will be donated into the Common Good Fund that will be solely committed to ending poverty on Earth.

The second program is a way for all parents to create a trust fund for each child at birth or at any time. If ten family members and friends (mom and dad, grandparents on both sides, two Godmothers, and two Godfathers) commit to donate $10 a month by electronic transfer (only one decision needed) for twenty years ($120 each a year per person), the capital can grow tax free using the Pooled Income Fund program of the IRS. The child can then receive a distribution every month from his or her eighteenth year on with the monthly distribution when elderly being the equivalent of the current average social security check in the US. This assumes that the stock market does on average as well as it has done for the last 89 years including the Great Depression of 1929: 10.3% a year. Upon death, the balance will go into the Common Good

Fund to end poverty. So, the ten-or-more people choosing to support an individual child know their capital is not only solely supporting that child for the rest of his or her life but upon death the balance will forever be used to end poverty on Earth. Also, any amount of additional capital can be donated to the child's trust at any time, especially on birthdays, at graduations, or at any time, including from wills.

*Article Twenty-Two:* The businesses owned by citizens will be encouraged to become members of the Common Good Business Association (CGBA). In doing so they commit to give priority to the common good—the maturation of the universe—and second priority to profit or anything else. Secondly, if they wish they can annually invest, not donate, a portion of annual profits if any in one or more common good investment funds. The latter solely focus on the development of common good businesses and in particular buying businesses and converting them into stage three common good businesses. Stage three common good businesses place a cap on their annual return to investors that is made public. If a startup it could be 1,000% a year. However, as it approaches being a mature business, its cap is somewhere lower than 15% annually. Any capital earned above this annual cap is also invested in common good investment funds. One of the goals of the latter is to provide a market rate return. Finally, if because of losses or the need to invest in its business the company needs this capital, it can borrow using it as collateral from anywhere including the common good investment funds. Since the return would be close to the cost of borrowing, the capital can be going in two directions at the same time. Also, if there is a need to provide for the promised return to investors in a year, the capital could be used as collateral to borrow the capital needed for this purpose as well and then repaid in future years when the return exceeds the promised return. These companies will be viewed as excellent investments by the investment community for that portion of client's portfolios seeking a steady and reasonable rate of return. Finally, the CGBA will also encourage the use of a sports league cooperative relationship among product market competitors. In the private sector they publicly and voluntarily agree on the "common good rules of play." They then have their financial auditors also monitor if these agreements are being kept, the equivalent of referees in sports leagues. In this way and fully in the private sector, capitalism can be matured into common good capitalism.

*Article Twenty-Three:* The CGN will never go into debt. It can launch programs where investors can participate, but it will not go into debt so there will never be a concern about the financial viability of the CGN.

*Article Twenty-Four:* Each Community, Elder Body, and Congress will have an Annual Meeting. To conduct business at least fifty percent of citizens or members must be present physically or electronically. Each Community, Elder Body, and Congress Board of Facilitators will usually meet once a month.

*Article Twenty-Five:* Using the consensus process in Article Nine, the first members of the Community's Elder Body are elected by the citizens of the Community at its Annual Meeting or at a special meeting at least partially for this purpose. From that point forward members of the Elder Body are chosen each year at the Annual Meeting of the Community with at least a majority of the Elder Body Board of Facilitators present. The approval to become a member of the Elder Body is a joint decision by the Community and Elder Body at this meeting using the consensus process described in Article Nine. If consensus cannot be reached, the decision can be by a two-thirds vote. However, every effort should be made to not use this default choice.

*Article Twenty-Six:* The Board of Facilitators of the Elder Bodies shall have at least six and best to have ten members. Serving two year terms, half will be up for election each year. They are chosen each year at the Elder Body Annual Meeting using the consensus process in Article Nine. Members of the Community can attend. If a person ceases to be a member of the Board of Facilitators for any reason and there is more than six months to the next Annual Meeting, the Elder Body Board of Facilitators can appoint a replacement for the remainder of that position's term. The Board of Facilitators can replace a member if absent for three consecutive meetings.

*Article Twenty-Seven:* The Board of Facilitators of the Communities and Congresses shall have at least six and best to have ten members. Serving two year terms, half will be up for election each year. They are chosen each year at their Annual Meetings using the consensus process in Article Nine. If a person ceases to be a member of the Board of Facilitators for any reason and there is more than six months to the next Annual Meeting, the Community or Congress Board of Facilitators, in consultation with the Board of Facilitators of their Elder Body, can appoint a replacement for the remainder of that position's term. A Board of Facilitators can replace a member if absent for three consecutive meetings.

*Article Twenty-Eight:* Amendments or additional Articles to this Constitution are only possible by a two-thirds voting decision of all the Community's, Congress's, and Elder Body's Boards of Facilitators after consultation with the citizens of their Communities at an Annual Meeting. Anyone can initiate an amendment. However, it can only be sent to all the Communities, Elder Bodies, and Congress Bodies Board of Facilitators for consideration if both the Boards of Facilitators of a Community and Elder Body after consultation with the Community at an Annual Meeting, agree by a two-thirds vote to bring it forward to the entire organization. Before this vote is taken there must be the use of Article Nine by both Bodies, either alone or together and possibly at the Annual Meeting of the Community, to first seek a consensus process decision.

# 3
# Why This Constitution at This Time?

AS STATED IN THE PREAMBLE, WE NOW KNOW that the human skill of self-consciousness is a skill, not the result of a biological mutation many years ago. This means it is not something like our lungs or liver that just comes into existence as part of our physical body's maturation. It is a skill that, like walking or riding a bicycle, we can get more skilled at doing. We can also reach full maturity at doing it to the point it is a habit that we do not have to think about anymore while we are doing it.

We are not born with it and, like learning the skill of walking or riding a bicycle, we learn it by mastering in a natural progression each smaller skill, turning it into a habit, and integrating the habits of all the smaller skills into one habit called "mature self-consciousness." We also know that like any skill there is a highest smaller skill of this total skill.

Finally, we also know that once this has been achieved and we discover there is not a higher smaller skill to learn, our maturation in the skill of self-consciousness is complete. We then discover that our priority is no longer our personal maturation of this skill but the maturation of the totality of who we are: the indivisible universe, our true total self. At that point, it is self-evident that the universe will not die but we will die. Also, that maturation is the fundamental process and priority of the universe. Then in action, maturation of the universe, our total self, becomes our highest priority. This is herein labeled "eldering."

We do not now know where this maturation process will take us in the many potential arrangements of the parts of the universe, but we do know that maturation is the fundamental process in nature. Finally, we also know that personal fulfillment, happiness, enlightenment, the state of grace, or whatever else we may choose to call it lies in freely choosing each moment to be a participant in its maturation process. As a result of knowing this and acting on it by giving priority in action to eldering we discover that the contented happiness we have been seeking is consistently available to us. Once we have this experience we know there is nothing new to learn to master this skill of self-consciousness. From wherever we are standing in the universe, the rest of our lives we love eldering, being a direct self-conscious participant in the maturation of it.

CGN is built on this worldview. It is for people who share it or intuitively know that they are on the path of mastering it and want to be with those also on this path. To learn the full worldview of this path, I recommend you read another book by me entitled *Eldering: What we do between enlightenment and death.*

The highest priority of this Constitution, of this agreement, is a commitment by all citizens who join to live according to this worldview.

*This is the unifying agreement that defines CGN as an agreement nation.*

You will also notice that the second priority is that each person is free to participate in any activity or program or not. CGN builds on the maturity of the teen layer of maturity which is respect for each individual's ability and right to exercise individual free choice. By extension you will also notice that no Body within CGN has the ability to enforce anything on any citizen except the keeping of agreements.

*Everything is based on making and keeping agreements. Human life is agreements. It is the other side of the coin of individual freedom that recognizes we are all in this together as parts of an indivisible whole.*

This is to both provide assurance to all citizens that their teen layer of maturity, their ability and right to exercise individual freedom of choice, will be fully honored and that any agreements made with others will be kept so we can enjoy being together. This will allow each to participate without fear. The CGN worldview also allows each citizen to participate in CGN with full trust in the primary good intentions of every other citizen. By the nature of the universe being an indivisible whole, we know this priority cannot be escaped

*Speaking from and to that place in each other will allow cooperative, caring, and co-creative behavior to flourish.*

Of course, once agreements are made by any citizen and he or she does not keep them, anyone or Body can insist they be kept. If they are not kept, the person's citizenship can be ended but only after a Clearing Process.

In all mutual activities, agreements are made and expected to be kept. The first action is always to ask anyone not keeping the agreements to keep them. Only when one does not keep agreements clearly made and continues to not keep them upon being notified that they are not being kept is it appropriate to take further action, such as calling for a Clearing Process.

The worldview defined in the Constitution is the one upon which the CGN is based. You may like some of it but not all of it. Then you should not choose to join it. This is for people who understand and embrace this worldview so we can focus our attention on building on it together to create the lives, relationships, communities of friends, and agreement nation we want. There will surely be discussions about parts of it and always the possibility for representing it in better ways, improving upon it, and amending it. Maturation is the fundamental process in nature. However, the current basic worldview needs to be embraced by all those who choose to be citizens of CGN so there is not the possibility of it unraveling as a result of the projection of less mature worldviews upon it. This has often been the problem of past organizations and why they are now experienced as far from what many believe their founders would support.

Next, you will notice that this worldview assumes cooperation, not competition, is the fundamental process in nature. It goes one step further and assumes that maturation is the particular kind of cooperation that is the fundamental process in nature. The assumption that competition is the fundamental process in nature is the result of it not being understood that both a human language and the skill of self-consciousness are skills. At the lower layers of maturity in the skill of self-consciousness the fundamental assumption in language, that the universe is an immense number of separate parts, is assumed to be accurate rather than known as a *mutually agreed upon illusion tool.* We now know it is easily self-evident in one's direct experience that *the universe is an indivisible whole.* However, to discover it there we each have to have the courage to keep our power and study our direct experience to witness it. We also know that the assumption in language that it is separate parts is a valuable tool because it allows us to be self-conscious parts of the indivisible universe, but it is a *mutually agreed upon illusion tool.*

Most people discover the universe is an indivisible whole by studying their breathing and noticing that they are not choosing to breath. They have been naturally and effortlessly breathing since coming out of the womb. If the Earth is not in the particular relationship it has with the universe, if it did not have the atmosphere it has instead of the atmosphere of Mars or Venus, if there was no air around us at all times, and if our physical bodies were not alive and healthy, we would not be able to breath. And if all of these parts were not in consistent full cooperation with each other, our physical bodies would not be breathing. Thus, we now know by keeping our power and studying our direct experience of breathing that the universe is an indivisible whole and it is doing our breathing. We also will die, but the universe will not die. Therefore, at full maturity in the skill of self-consciousness we naturally, effortlessly, and freely choose to give priority to the maturation of the universe, the common good. In one way or another this has been defined as moral behavior throughout history. Thus, the highest behavioral priority of the CGN is moral behavior. It is also accurately seen as natural when full maturity has been achieved in the skill of self-consciousness.

*A paternalistic system is not necessary to force people to be moral in their behavior when they have achieved full maturity in the skill of self-consciousness. Therefore, the highest priority of CGN is to elder people, or assist people in self-eldering themselves, up the last layers to full maturity in the skill of self-consciousness.*

Next, you will notice that herein we are only speaking to the beliefs in the skill of self-consciousness. It is emphasized that anyone can give priority to any religious, philosophical, scientific, or other belief one chooses. This constitution is based on the humble position that we do not know the ultimate answer to the mysteries still not understood about the operation of the universe.

At the same time, we do know that it is self-evident that maturation is the fundamental process in nature. We are going somewhere in the oneness of nature: the universe is maturing. It is also obvious that the oneness of nature is the only thing that is real. All else is human language. We also know from direct experience that the consistent experience of contented happiness is possible by giving priority in our actions to eldering, direct self-conscious participation in the maturation of the universe. The self-interest of the universe is now our self-interest. This provides the contented personal happiness we have intuitively known as our birthright since being on the path of mastering the skill of self-consciousness.

In Article One you will notice that the highest activity priority of this agreement nation is the eldering of our children to full maturity in the skill of self-consciousness before they enter their twenties.

*This is the only permanent solution to all the immaturities we experience on Earth.*

It is pointed out that when all children are well eldered into the mastery of this skill, there will no longer be a need for armaments. There will no longer be wars. There will no longer be killing and thievery. We are a long way from this now, but we can now see that eldering our children and each other to full maturity in the skill of self-consciousness is the key to all the people on Earth getting there.

To make this easier to accomplish, in Article Four all are encouraged to invite friends to join in forming Communities, not necessarily people living on the same contiguous land but usually those living in the same local area. The primary purpose of these Communities is to elder ourselves, each other, and our children to full maturity in the skill of self-consciousness. Particularly as parents, not being alone in this process with one's children can make it much easier to accomplish. Secondly, an intimate community of friends is fun. It is safe. It is nurturing. It is playful. It seeks and finds wisdom together from a place of mutual respect, from a place of speaking from and to the natural highest priority in each of us being the common good. This is why these Communities are the fundamental building blocks of CGN.

Of course, existing communities of friends, such as religious congregations, workplaces, and relatives where all or some choose to join the CGN, can be their Community.

It is these Communities that choose the first members of the Elder Body and both then elect a Board of Facilitators of the Community. The Boards of

Facilitators of the Elder Body and Community each elect two representatives from their Boards to the Local Association Elder Body and Congress.

It is very important today to have people who know each other choosing their leaders. Otherwise marketing, trickery, fake news, manipulation, and all kinds of other immature behaviors can affect one's thinking. Secondly, elections are through a consensus process rather than by majority votes, a competitive process. This consensus election process was described in Article Nine.

*The priority is always a genuine search for truth together, both in choosing the best people for positions and in the making of agreements. This is the opposite of giving priority to winning.*

Communities are different from having friends over for a party. Communities have an agreement to be together as a community and accept the responsibilities of it. It can be strongly organized or lightly organized, but it is organized. What and how it does what it does is fully up to it. Its only responsibility to the rest of the CGN is the election of two representatives from its Elder Body's Board of Facilitators to the Local Association Elder Body and two representatives by its Community Board of Facilitators to the Local Association Congress Body. The priority is to have no one feel pressured or fear pressure.

*This will have the primary attention of all be on how they can participate in the maturation of us all.*

In Article Eight it is described how the Elder Body has the ultimate power, delegates it to the Community or Congress, maintains the right to veto any decision, and will try to never exercise its veto power. Since the highest priority of the CGN is making sure all decisions by the community give priority to participation in the maturation of us all, this is institutionalized with the creation of the Elder Bodies. It's second priority is to assist all parents and each other in eldering the children and each other to full maturity in the skill of self-consciousness as early in their/our lives as possible.

This allows the Community's or Congress's Board of Facilitators to focus on the operations of the organization with the Elder Body's Board of Facilitators ready to assist them if they get caught up in it to the point where they need assistance to be sure the priority is the maturation of us all.

The relationship between the two is clearly laid out in a contractual form. At each level the Elder Body's Board of Facilitators has the ultimate authority, delegates fully responsibility to running the organization at that level to the Community or Congress, maintains the right to veto any decision, and tries to never exercise its veto power.

*The Elder Body's Board of Facilitators is in a relationship of assistance to the Congress.*

If the Elder Body Board of Facilitators ever needs to exercise its veto power, it has failed in its role of facilitating mature decisions within the Community or Congress. They know the Elder Body's Board of Facilitators is at all times watching from right in front of them to be sure they do not lose sight of their highest priority. The Elder Body's Board of Facilitators has a mechanism for monitoring the decisions of the Community or Congress, having two representatives sitting as *ex officio members* (without vote) of the Community's or Congress's Board of Facilitators at all times and able to call for a meeting with the Elder Body Board of Facilitators anytime they think it would be helpful. If it thinks it is necessary, as an ultimate action the Elder Body Board of Facilitators can call for a replacement of all the members of the Board of Facilitators of the Community or Congress.

This provides a safety valve known by the entire citizenry and it is there only as a safety valve. It is hoped it will never be used. However, it provides comfort for the citizenry. They know that if things become fully inappropriate and appear beyond being redeemed, action can occur to end it.

Article Nine indicates that when choosing leaders or representatives, the purpose of the process is to have all judge that the priority was in each case what was best for the Community or Association and by extension the maturation of the universe. By having people both volunteer and be asked to serve, all the people who could be best for the role sit in the center of the circle. The rest of the process was described in Article Nine.

The purpose of this process is to assure that all are emotionally involved and invested in the choice. It is also to have it ultimately experienced as a consensus rather than competitive process. This usually results in strong support for the candidate and the chosen person feeling strongly supported to serve in the role.

Article Ten describes a cooperative rather competitive process to resolve differences. Those with the difference, whether two or more individuals or two or more groups, are invited to use the Clearing Process. It was described in this Article. Again, the goal is to have the highest priority be our maturation and the maturation of us all through a cooperative, mutually respectful, and loving process rather than a competitive process.

Article Twelve indicates that each of the Communities, Congresses, and Elder Bodies has a Board of Facilitators and Chair. However, these Boards' job is not to make decisions and make others honor them. Quite the opposite. Its job is to identify needs not met and wants that are emergent, name them, and develop programs that many or an appropriate group of citizens will support as a response to these needs or wants. Any citizen is always free to participate or not participate in any activity of CGN. Thus, programs must be artfully designed so citizens easily see the value of them and want to participate as an expression of their desire to be a strong participant in the maturation of us all.

Also in Article Twelve it also states there will not be term limits. The responsibility is then placed mutually on the person and Body for giving priority to the best person for the position without another issue being dominant.

Article Thirteen indicates that there may be times when members of any Body want to speak without the fear of being misunderstood and for the safety of some or all. In these cases, by a majority vote, discussions can be kept confidential and not reported in the records of the meetings that are shared with all. However, as stated, all decisions must be reported.

Article Fourteen indicates that citizens filling positions can be financially compensated. This is not a process for gaining wealth. The compensation should be reasonable and error on the side of frugality rather than excess. The goal is to have each person receive at least a livable wage and be appropriately compensated at a reasonable level for the job being done, with "reasonable" and "appropriate" to be determined by those making the decision. Since the CGN will never go into debt, payments for services must be available or services are voluntary and not compensated.

Article Fifteen indicates that anyone serving in any role in CGN can be removed without cause. This is to assure mutually respectful behavior by those in the Body and ease at sustaining the priority of mutual maturation. That is why it is without cause.

Most of us have probably been on boards where a person's consistent immature behavior has been disruptive. The distaste for requesting that it stop, especially when it does not appear the person is capable of stopping it, consistently disrupts the group's ability to have its process be open, mutually respectful, caring, and co-creative. This option allows a high standard to be sustained.

Article Eighteen indicates that organizations, but not geographic nation government organizations, are welcome to join as organizational members. In doing so they are declaring that their highest priority is the maturation of the universe and any other priority, such as profit for shareholders or a particular mission, is second in priority.

There will be many ways they will judge wise to self-organize themselves in support of the mission of the CGN. The only check on this is if any Congress's or Elder Body's Board of Facilitators at any level has an issue with it. This can then be resolved using the Clearing Process.

Groups within geographic nations are not allowed to join simply to keep it clear that this is an agreement nation, not a geographic nation. This can prevent any creeping movement to have the actual priority in behavior be in support of any particular geographic nation and involved in the differences inside, between or among them. CGN is always seeking ways to support the operations of the geographic nations, but becoming part of any one of them is not its choice.

Article Twenty encourages the creation of an honest currency equivalent and possibly a digital currency. The latter can also serve as an equity equivalent to grow the CGN. There is no reason to have our currency losing value when an honest currency equivalent can be created. However, until there is a currency crisis there may not be a high demand for it. If that does occur, the CGN nation should be ready to make it available. Secondly, a digital currency could be used for the same purpose or as an equity equivalent, to raise money for projects that will increase the value of the digital currency and thereby provide a financial return to the investor.

Article Twenty-One speaks to the high priority the CGN gives to the ending of poverty on Earth.

Article Twenty-Two speaks to the need to mature our business community out of giving priority to private gain to giving priority to the common good and second priority to private gain or anything else. We do not want to do away with individual freedom and free markets. They honor the teen layer of maturity in the skill of self-consciousness. Therefore, the only way to accomplish this in the private sector is for citizens to commit to giving priority in their businesses to the actions described in Article Twenty-Two. To learn more about common good capitalism, read my book *Common Good Capitalism Is Inevitable.*

Finally, in Article Twenty-Three it was stated that the CGN will never go into debt. This will have all trust and respect it rather than become concerned about its financial viability.

*Trust is the most important ingredient to make sure all love being citizens of the CGN.*

This will not preclude it from accepting equity or bond donations or from taking equity, bond, or other financial positions using money provided by others. It will also not preclude it from raising capital using equity, bond, or the use of other methods and investing it in projects in alignment with its priority. In the USA, the CGN can be a 501(c)(3) public tax-exempt charitable and educational organization and receive donations of capital or securities where the donors receive a tax deduction. If the CGN is not a 501 (c)(3) organization, it can create one as a sister organization to serve charitable, educational, literary, scientific research, and all other programs permitted by 501(c)(3) organizations. If it is a 501(c)(3), it can create for-profit organizations where it is a substantial owner of their shares, if necessary using a 501(c)(4) legislation to do so.

Article Twenty-Eight declares, in part, that amendments to this Constitution are only possible by a two-thirds voting decision of all the Communities', Congresses' and Elder Bodies' Boards of Facilitators after consultation with the members of their Communities at an Annual Meeting. The rest of the process described here is to assure that there is serious consideration before amendments can be brought forward and brought to a vote, and then only after Article Nine is used to seek a consensus decision.

In summary, this is a living document. It is based on respect for each person's ability and right to exercise independent free choice and make and keep agreements. It avoids paternalistic processes. Its highest priority, of giving priority in all behaviors to the best actions that are participation in the maturation of the universe, is institutionalized in the Elder Body. There is also a process for managing, changing, and resolving disagreements.

Most important, it recognizes there is nothing more important both for us as individuals and us all than for each of us to achieve full maturity in the skill of self-consciousness as early in life as possible.

# 4
# Common Good Nation Worldview

THIS AGREEMENT NATION IS BASED ON A WORLDVIEW, some fundamental assumptions about reality and our lives.

*The fundamental assumption of the CGN is that the universe is an indivisible whole.*

The *second assumption* is that our human languages are based on the exact opposite assumption: that the universe is an immense number of separate parts.

The *third assumption* is that mastering the relationship between our use of a human language (separate parts) and the oneness of nature is a skill, the skill of self-consciousness.

We are not born with it. We learn it the same way we learn any other skill, such as riding a bicycle. There are smaller skills we learn in a natural progression, there is a highest smaller skill, and when we have learned all of them and integrated them together into one mature skill and habit we have reached full maturity in the skill of riding a bicycle.

It is the same when mastering the skill of self-consciousness.

The *fourth assumption* is that all things are conscious: they are each being one thing rather than another. Human beings through the invention of human languages are able to master the skill of self-consciousness: knowing what we are doing while we are doing it. We are also able to exercise free choice to continue doing it or not. Unlike a dog or horse, rather than just reacting we can be the watchers and choosers, what we label "the exercise of free choice." Self-consciousness also allows us to analyze the past, plan for the future, and consistently execute a plan in the present. It also allows us to change our self-definition as we mature up each smaller skill of self-consciousness to include it.

These are the first four of the five basic assumptions of the Common Good Worldview that is the foundation of CGN. What is most significant about them is that they are based on the assumption that self-consciousness is a skill.

For the last many decades, it has been believed in linguistic science that self-consciousness in human beings was the result of a biological mutation hundreds of thousands of years ago. Like our kidneys, lungs, and livers, it was something that was part of our physical bodies and any maturity was primarily the result of biological activity.

*We now know this is not true. We now know it is a skill we can learn, get better at, and achieve full maturity in executing it as a skill.*

We are not born with it and it does not come into existence biologically. We learn it by mastering a smaller skill that builds upon the previous smaller skill in a natural progression. Most important, there is a highest smaller skill that results in full maturity in the skill of self-consciousness. Even more important, we can all be eldered into mastering the full skill by the time we leave our teen years.

Between mastering this skill and death we have the same highest priority in our actions, what is herein labeled "eldering." It is not defined by age. As stated above, we can master the skill of self-consciousness and be consistently giving priority to eldering by the time we are leaving our teen years.

Eldering is our consistent priority in relationships once we have mastered full maturity in the skill of self-consciousness. It is each moment doing whatever we each judge to be our best action for the maturation of the universe. We quickly discover that this priority in action provides us the consistent experience of contented happiness we have intuitively known all along is our birthright.

The *fifth assumption* is that the universe is going somewhere in the reality of the oneness of nature. It is maturing.

If the universe is an indivisible whole, then all the perceived parts are cooperating for the good of the one whole. What is the good of the one whole? It is self-evident that on the whole each generation has the ability to be more mature than the last generation. We each also mature.

When we each learn to walk, we do not go back to crawling. When we each learn to use chopsticks with one hand we do not go back to using them with two hands. Maturation is the fundamental process in nature.

We are not born with the skill of self-consciousness, but as we master each smaller skill in the natural progression we do not easily go back to giving priority to the priority of a lower layer. We discover that life is more enjoyable when we discover each of the following seven skills in this order: sensations, recognizing differences, knowing how to speak a human language, exercise free choice, experiencing our lives being meaningful as the result of living according to a freely chosen worldview, discovering the accurate worldview, and learning to give priority to the experience of the oneness of nature so we keep our power rather than give it to a belief and then obey it the rest of our lives.

*A belief is a second thing that only exists in the mutually agreed upon illusion tool of separate parts.*

It is obvious that we are each maturing at all times, either in the skill of self-consciousness or the skill of eldering. The universe is also maturing. It is maturing in the only reality there is: the oneness of nature. People 2000 years ago could not have imagined electricity and smartphones, and we cannot easily imagine the new more cooperative relationships we will discover how to orchestrate with the parts of the universe to more beautifully meet our needs 2000 years in the future. However, there is one constant that we do know will always be present: we, the universe, will be maturing.

Maturation is different from evolution. Evolution describes how things change. Maturation describes why they are changing: the universe is maturing. We are going somewhere, not primarily in the mutually agreed upon illusions of human language's separate parts. We are going somewhere relative to where we have been in the reality of oneness.

*Usually nothing physically changes but we have found more mature ways to facilitate relationships among the parts.*

When we have mastered the full skill of self-consciousness and focus on eldering, we are able to experience happiness as the consistent container of all we experience, often called "enlightenment," "the state of grace," "fulfillment," and with many other names. They all name the skill of being able to sustain this experience of contented happiness as the container of all that we experience.

We also discover that there is only one priority in our actions that sustains this experience: eldering. If the universe is an indivisible whole, then you, me, and all of us are it. We are actually walking around inside ourself talking to ourself. It is our human language that, at the lower layers of maturity of the skill of self-consciousness, has us think we are each a part separate from all else. We are no more a separate part than our kidney is separate from our physical body. This is understood when the highest layer of maturity in the skill of self-consciousness has been mastered. We then know that the self-interest of the universe is actually our self-interest. Eldering is the act of honoring this fact. Thus, eldering is giving priority to being the universe that will not die, and second priority to being our physical body that will die. It is living in reality. That is why it results in the consistent feeling of contented happiness.

People throughout history have discovered the same fundamental truths. What has been missing up until recently has been two things: 1) the knowledge that self-consciousness is a skill, and 2) understanding the relationship between a human language (separate parts as a mutually agreed upon illusion tool) and the oneness of nature (reality). We now know both. CGN is based on this knowledge.

It is easily self-evident that the universe is an indivisible whole. In my book, *Eldering: What we do between enlightenment and death,* I guide readers in a study of their breathing to the point of discovering that it is the universe that is doing our breathing. We are not self-consciously breathing and we have been breathing since birth. The question becomes, "Who or what is doing our breathing?" We discover that if the Earth was not in the particular relationship it is in with the universe, it would not have the atmosphere that allows us to breath. If for fifteen minutes our lungs, our healthy physical bodies, and Earth's atmosphere are not at all times doing what each are doing, we would not be able to breath. By keeping our power and studying our breathing, it is obvious that the universe is an indivisible whole where all the parts are in a constant state of cooperation with each other.

However, to come to know this as true in a way that we will never forget it or allow ourselves to move against it, we each have to have the courage to keep our power: from the inside no one else can move our arms and legs or think our thoughts. Also, if we do not yet understand the relationship between our human languages and the oneness of nature, we will easily and unconsciously remain operating at one of the lower layers of maturity of the skill of self-consciousness that assumes separate parts are real and we are each one of them. This is where we easily give our power to a second thing that does not exist: another person, an organization, or a belief in words.

No one takes our power from us. At the lower layers of maturity of the skill of self-consciousness we give it away without knowing we are doing it. Part of reaching maturity in the skill of self-consciousness is learning how to not do that anymore.

We grow up dependent upon our parents for survival. We are in the pattern of giving our power to them to survive. Later we give our power to other people, organizations, and beliefs. Examples are coaches, businesses, and statements in words we call "beliefs." Each of these is a part of the universe we are treating as if it is a separate part. This is the result of still unconsciously operating as if the assumption that allows us to create a human language and become self-conscious is accurate. It is not.

*To keep our power, we need to give priority to our direct experience.*

We can't learn to ride a bicycle without a bicycle. We need the direct experience of working with it to learn the skill of riding it. This is giving priority to direct experience to learn a skill.

This is what we also need to do to achieve full maturity in the skill of self-consciousness. We need to keep our power and go to our direct experience to learn each smaller skill in the natural progression as a skill. Like learning the skill of riding a bicycle in direct experience, it then becomes a habit and part of who we are without having to choose it or think about it anymore.

*This is maturation in action.*

When we learn how to launch a satellite, that is also maturation in action. When we learn how to move from dictatorship to democracy, that is also maturation in action. Nothing in the parts of the universe has changed. What has changed is our ability to co-ordinate them together in new ways and in the making of new things and relationships that are a maturation of the universe.

The human skill of self-consciousness is a maturation of the universe that allows it to be self-consciously present in billions of places on Earth at the same time and surely someday throughout the universe.

*It is obvious that we mature. It is now obvious that the indivisible universe also matures.*

At the teen layer, we discover that we have the ability and right of exercising individual free choice. Our brains are not sufficiently developed to fully understand this until our teen years. At the next layer, the adult layer, we discover that our most important free choice is our worldview. We want our lives to be meaningful. That means we need to have a reason for doing one thing rather than another. This necessitates choosing a fundamental worldview to guide us in those choices.

We usually choose one from the many we come upon. Often, we just accept the one in which we grew up. It could be a religion, business approach to life, a philosophy of choice, a scientific perspective, or any worldview we decide gives our lives meaning.

At the discovery of each next smaller skill we are happier than we were before and get very excited. But eventually the excitement wears off when we realized we are not consistently experiencing the effortless and contented happiness we intuitively know is our birthright. We then search for the next smaller skill and eventually can discover the next layer of the skill of self-consciousness.

The next layer, the elder layer, is the discovery of the accurate fundamental worldview, that the universe is an indivisible whole. However, we are so used to choosing a belief in words as our highest priority that we again do it.

*This is where our recent discovery that self-consciousness is a skill becomes important.*

Words are a mutually agreed upon illusion tool we invented so we can be self-conscious. They are a tool solely for that purpose. However, at the lower layers of maturity in the skill of self-consciousness we act as if this tool's fundamental assumption about reality is accurate, that the universe is an immense number of separate parts and we are each one of them.

*There are parts but there are not separate parts, except in the mutually agreed upon illusion tool of a human language.*

At the highest layer, the mature elder layer, we discover we are still giving our power to a second thing and we no longer believe there is a second thing to receive our power.

*We are still giving priority to words, to some of those mutually agreed upon illusion tools we invented.*

Discovering we have still not found the consistent experience of the contented happiness we know as our birthright, we search further. We can eventually discover that there is only one way to escape giving our power to an illusionary separate part: we have to give priority to the *experience* of the oneness of nature. Experience includes everything, including our physical body. So, we are not giving our power to a second thing.

There is no boundary to experience. It has no edge. It has no beginning point. It has no end point. It does not have time. Thus, the experience of being our physical body is actually the experience of being the universe. When less mature, and thinking we are only our physical body, we only look for information from it. Now we know we can receive information directly from the universe, the rest of our physical body. People usually refer to this information as "intuition," "a gut feeling," "the little voice within," and many other names.

Therefore, it is also obvious that our highest priority is not the interests of our physical body but the interests of the universe. Our second priority is our physical body because it is the only part of the universe where from the inside we have sole and complete control. However, just as a butterfly is first a caterpillar and later a butterfly, we first operate as if the fundamental assumption in language that the universe is an immense number of separate parts and we are each one of them is accurate. Only later do we discover the universe is an indivisible whole.

*This full maturation in the skill of self-consciousness was just the beginning of our lives, not an end to seek.*

Now our highest priority is not our personal maturation. It is complete. Now our highest priority is the maturation of the universe, the totality of who we are. We discover that when we give it priority in our actions, we are happy. More important, when we consistently do it we are consistently happy. A happiness that has no degrees of being happy. It is the effortlessly and contented happiness we knew as a toddler when we had received the milk or anything else we needed. There are no degrees of it. It is the contented happiness that has no degrees of experiencing it.

*It is the only feeling that does not have degrees of feeling it.*

All other feelings are relative feelings, feelings between our physical bodies and another person or part of the universe. This feeling, the feeling that is the result of giving priority each moment to the maturation of the universe, is the only feeling that does not have degrees of feeling it. Therefore, we can't get better or worse at it. All we can do is hang out in it as the chosen experiential container of all else we experience. Since this is self-consciously living moment to moment in reality, it is irresistible. In our actions, we give it priority the rest of our lives. Herein this is labeled "eldering."

*We now know that we are self-conscious participants in the fundamental process of the universe: maturation. That is what we need to know to freely choose the consistent experience of contented happiness as the container of all else we experience.*

This is the worldview upon which the CGN is based. Thus, one of our highest priorities is raising our children to full maturity in the skill of self-consciousness before they leave home and marry. Achieving this is the only permanent solution to all the immature behaviors we experience and the source of all conflicts.

*Finally, it is important to point out that this worldview is part of mastering the skill of self-consciousness to become fully mature human beings. There is still much about understanding the operations of the universe we do not know.*

This worldview accepts the humble position that we do not know many things about it. Therefore, it also accepts that people will give priority to beliefs above the beliefs necessary to master the skill of self-consciousness, what might be called "super beliefs." It could be a religious, philosophical, scientific, or any other belief one chooses. The CGN is solely focused on bringing people together who understand there are layers of maturity of the skill of self-consciousness, we can master it as a skill, and we can then enjoy the pleasure of giving priority to eldering the rest of our lives. Above the mastery of this skill, any citizen can give priority to any "super belief" he or she chooses.

CGN is based on the mastery of a skill, the skill of human self-consciousness.

# 5
# Communities

IT IS VALUABLE TO REMEMBER THAT IT IS OUR HUMAN languages that allow us to be self-conscious. It is also far more enjoyable to live in this self-conscious experience than to simply be reacting to things. That was all we could do before we invented our human languages and became self-conscious.

Throwing the ball and having Fido run and get it and bring it back to us easily gets boring. However, we can play a pickup game of basketball all day and be enjoying it. When playing basketball, we are mutually choosing and agreeing to live inside some agreements: the rules of the game.

*We are relating self-consciously. It is living within some agreements.*

Our highest priority when playing basketball is honoring the rules of the game. Our second priority is to play it well, get better at it, and enjoy relating within some agreements. This is far more enjoyable than again throwing the ball for Fido.

Relating self-consciously is moving as one together, whether it is playing the game of basketball, being married, being part of a business, being part of a democracy, or doing anything with others based upon agreements.

*That is what self-consciousness is. It is agreements.*

First the agreement to be using some sounds and symbols, called "a particular human language." Secondly the agreement to be living according to what we believe is true. Thirdly, and if we have reached full maturity in the skill of self-consciousness, the agreement with ourselves that we are first the universe that will not die and secondly our physical bodies that will die.

*Each moment this allows us to move as one with all that exists and know we are doing it while we are doing it. This is far more enjoyable than just reacting to the things around us.*

The most thorough experience of moving as one is marriage and raising children. The second most thorough experience of moving as one is having our marriages be joined together into a village. Thus, throughout history human beings have formed marriages and villages as the most important agreements in their lives.

When we have reached full maturity in the skill of self-consciousness, we naturally marry as equals and without the need of vows to assure we will remain married. When we have not reached full maturity in this skill, there is always a paternalistic system, for instance, an outside action to make sure our marriages stay together.

When dealing with the reality that most of the young people in the village are not operating at the highest layer of maturity of the skill of self-consciousness, the elders at the time may see the necessity, for the health of the children and the whole village, to insist upon marriage vows.

A paternalistic system is then instituted. Paternalism is where we give our power to another person, organization, or belief and then have a relationship of obedience to it.

*Common Good Communities are based on the replacement of paternalistic systems with agreements and the keeping of agreements between and among equals.*

At a minimum, these agreements are an honoring of the teen layer of maturity, our ability and right of exercising individual free choice. The two people in marriage are also committed to self-eldering and the eldering of each other to full maturity in the skill of self-consciousness. It is known that this priority is the only priority that is simultaneously best for each and all without any experience of conflict between personal self-interest and the common good.

We are now at a time in the maturation of human beings when it is possible to elder our children to full maturity in the skill of self-consciousness before they leave home. Those who have achieved it will not need vows to know their marriages will remain together. They know they will continue to give priority to mutually living in the full maturity of the skill of self-consciousness. This is self-evident: it is a consistent joy to remain there together. Thus, not only will a paternalistic system not be necessary for them to continue living together, they do not want to be part of a paternalistic system.

*They do not want to give their power to a second thing and obey it.*

My parents clearly stayed together because they had taken a vow of marriage. Many people today live together without getting married, later get married, and if it is judged best end their marriages. When my Aunt Anna could no longer remain in her marriage, at ten years old I went with my mother to sneak her out of town at night and set her life up in another town. We could not allow the world to know that one of our relatives had separated from her husband. The paternalistic system was most important. I can still see the deep look of shame on my Aunt Anna's face.

Today my friends and I easily live with our partners for long periods of time without getting married, get married, and get divorced if it is no longer a fulfilling experience. This reveals that our priority is at least the teen layer of at all times honoring our ability and right of individual free choice.

The next generations are going to be discovering the last few layers of maturity of the skill of self-consciousness. This will probably still result in marriages, marriages without vows. They will exist to celebrate the fact that they have together achieved the highest layer of maturity of the skill of self-consciousness as the foundation of their relationship. They also want their community of family and friends to join with them in a celebratory ritual that honors this fact.

This will be a very different marriage ceremony than the ones my parents experienced. It will be the honoring of the *mutual knowledge and skill* of the highest layer of maturity of the skill of self-consciousness. It will not be operating at the child layer where either our parents decide who we will each marry or we each decide ourselves with the priority being to have some wants satisfied, wants such as companionship, sex, and/or having children.

Throughout history when societies witnessed young people operating at this child or teen layer of maturity, for the good of the community it developed marriage vows. For the good of the community, they wanted to make sure the couples stayed together.

As we go forward, for many couples this will no longer be acceptable. As many have recently done, they will still go through the marriage ceremony with the vows to honor the desires of their parents. However, for them the priority will be the above.

It is also true that many of today's marriages have ended up in divorce or living parallel lives while remaining married. Although they are honoring the teen layer and often also the adult layer of maturity in the skill of self-consciousness, they have not been living together at the mature elder layer, the highest layer. This usually results in a want (child layer), desire for more individual freedom (teen layer), or changed worldview (adult layer) becoming more important and the marriage ending up in divorce. The want could be to give priority to raising the children that ends giving priority to sustaining the experience of mature elder love as the container of this activity. The desire for more *freedom* could be a desire to explore relationships with other partners. The reason for leaving could be a change in one's way of thinking, one's *worldview.*

In the absence of having mastered the last layers of maturity in the skill of self-consciousness, it will usually be because for at least one of the parties the highest priority of one of the lower layers of maturity became more important. Not being aware there are layers of maturity of the skill of self-consciousness, they did not know that instead of divorce they could join in mutually self-eldering themselves up the last layers of maturity of the skill of self-consciousness.

As people learn to do this, they will naturally, effortlessly, and freely remain together for the joy of moving intimately with one other person at the highest layer of maturity of the skill of self-consciousness and for no other reason. They will raise their children together to enjoy eldering them within the container of this mature relationship love and to full maturity in the skill of self-consciousness before they leave home. They know this is their highest priority in raising them. They will also each support the other's ways of participating in the maturation of us all through their eldering activities in the community.

In Common Good Communities, there is an agreement that there are layers of maturity of the skill of self-consciousness and a highest layer we can master before we reach our twenties. It is based on the fact that the universe is an indivisible whole. Other than this, how each of these communities will form is fully and solely up to the people creating them.

The most natural process will be for friends who have come to understand this to turn their friendships into a community where they will be formally operating according to this knowledge. They may each still have different super beliefs, a belief that is more important to them than the mastery of the skill of self-consciousness. Their super belief could be a religious, philosophical, scientific, or any other belief about the universe and our place in it. However, at a minimum they agree that mastering the *skill* of self-consciousness is the natural priority of a human life regardless of what each person chooses as his or her super belief.

The other way communities can become defined as Common Good Communities is to include it as an additional part of an existing community. The existing community could be the congregation of a church, temple, or synagogue. It could be an existing non-profit, membership, or cooperative organization. It could be an existing business. Some but not all the members of these existing groups could choose to also become a CGN Community.

It is the acknowledgement by the group of two things:

### *Common Good Community Agreement*

1. There are layers of maturity of the skill of self-consciousness, we can master this skill by the time we are in our twenties, and the most fundamental belief in the skill of self-consciousness is that the universe is an indivisible whole. And,
2. We choose to constitute ourselves as a Community within the Common Good Nation.

Of course, a person could choose to join the CGN as an individual, join or form a Community later, or remain an individual member. However, individual members will not be able to participate in the governance of CGN. This is to encourage all to become members of a Community, one of the most important agreement foundations of a person's life.

When a person honors that there are layers of maturity of the skill of self-consciousness and that the most fundamental belief to achieve mastery of this skill is that the universe is an indivisible whole, one naturally, effortlessly, and freely chooses to become fully mature in this skill. Nothing else is needed.

*Nature moving through us will take care of the rest without the need for a paternalistic system. Instead there is an honoring of our freely chosen agreements with each other.*

We will also each do our best to self-elder ourselves to full maturity in the skill of self-consciousness. And we will joyfully keep our agreements with each other as an expression both of our maturity in this human skill and our love for one another.

The choice to become a Common Good Community within the CGN is a choice to join with the others who share this knowledge as part of your community's participation in the maturation of us all. Common Good Communities can do any and all things they choose that they judge are part of our participation in this.

For instance, for children entering each of the early layers of maturity, they can develop rituals that honor each child's maturity into it. At the higher layers, they can honor that each child is judged as ready to understand and embrace each of the higher layers that can only be achieved through self-eldering.

They can have parties of all kinds. They can organize sub-groups of all kinds, such as men's groups, women's groups, couples' groups, music playing groups, business support groups, entrepreneurial groups, political action groups, and any other kind of sub-groups they choose.

The purpose of the Common Good Community is this:

### *Common Good Community Purpose*

1. To be a Common Good Community in CGN, and
2. To keep our agreements.

The foundation of human life is the agreement to use a particular human language that allows us to live self-conscious lives together. Thus, the essence of human life is living in agreements with each other. Mature joy lies in living within agreements, first with ourselves and secondly with others.

We are free to make whatever agreements we choose, but once we make them we need to keep them or we have ceased living as human beings. As much as possible we want to manage the keeping of our agreements in a mutual respectful rather than paternalistic way. Therefore, when there are disagreements, especially around the breaking of an agreement, we want to use what is called herein a "Clearing Process." This is where the two parties in disagreement choose by agreement some people to facilitate a resolution of the disagreement, conflict, or not keeping of agreements. The basic format for a Clearing Process was described in the Constitution.

The main point is that priority is given to a cooperative process toward the making and keeping of agreements rather than any form of competition or paternalistic process. The priority in the CGN is to resolve differences through a Clearing Process and the formation of new agreements if appropriate.

*Secondly, the honoring of individual freedom of choice cannot be uncoupled from our responsibility to keep agreements. They are two sides of the same coin.*

Human life is agreement life. It begins with the agreement on a human language and extends into nearly every layer of maturity as, fundamentally, the making and keeping of agreements with ourselves as we discover each smaller skill of the layers of maturity of self-consciousness.

The goal of the Common Good Community is to only make agreements that are in alignment with the maturation of the universe. That is the fundamental process in nature and personal happiness lies in being consistently in alignment with it. The second goal is to resolve all differences using mutual respect and additional agreements instead of competitive or paternalistic systems. It is also important to note that, as when raising children, there are times and places where healthy paternalistic processes are appropriate.

To know when it is appropriate, it is important to understand hierarchy.

It is always present in self-conscious activities: there is always prioritization since we can only do one thing at a time. At the same time, hierarchy must always be second in priority to participating in the maturation of us all.

*A hierarchical system is primarily an efficiency system, not a power system.*

If there is a party in my house and a fire breaks out, we will all want me to lead us to the basement door to get out of the house. The priority is efficiency. People giving their power to me is secondary.

The Mondragon Enterprises in the Basque region of Spain understand this well. They are an association of over 200 employee-owned enterprises and one of the largest conglomerates in Spain with hundreds of thousands of employee-owners in enterprises producing refrigerators, stoves, and construction equipment. There is also a cooperative health care system, bank, many grade schools, high schools, a university, farms, and consumer cooperatives. Each cooperative has a very clear hierarchical system of management. They see it as primarily an efficiency system.

The employee-owners in each enterprise know they have the ultimate power in it. However, once organized they want it to operate very hierarchically, with very few levels of it, for the efficiency it provides. The CEO of each enterprise is also free to operate it as he or she judges best. The meeting of the Management Committee (representatives from throughout the cooperatve) each Monday morning can make recommendations but not tell the CEO what to do. Otherwise there would be no ability to evaluate the CEO's performance. They can only remove him or her. Secondly, he or she was hired because the person is judged to know how to successfully run the enterprise within an employee-owned structure. There is no fear of dictatorial behavior. It is known by all that the employee-owners have the ultimate power.

It is also known by all that the highest priority of the employee-owned company is not the interests of the employee-owners. That is secondary. The highest priority is the common good, mainly the creation of additional employee-owned jobs where the priority is the common good. Mondragon knows hierarchy cannot be escaped. By having their priority institutionalized as the common good, they embrace hierarchy for its efficiency.

In paternalistic systems, like many in the USA, people *primarily* experience hierarchy as a power system. This is an immature understanding of hierarchy. At full maturity in the skill of self-consciousness, like the members of the Mondragon Cooperatives, we want to use hierarchical systems for their efficiency. We also want to make sure that any inappropriate or unfair relating as a result is able to be fully responded to and corrected to where there is mutual satisfaction using the Clearing Process.

As long as the priority in a Common Good Community is self-eldering and the eldering of each other to full maturity in the skill of self-consciousness, hierarchical systems of management can be joyfully used because they are an efficient way to execute a plan or run a business.

*In Common Good Communities, the priority among equals is agreement making and the keeping of agreements. The hierarchical structures that are always present in self-conscious activity are always second in priority to mutually and equally giving priority to the common good, the maturation of the universe.*

In summary, freely chosen Common Good Communities are the foundation of CGN. They honor that there are layers of maturity of the skill of self-consciousness, we can master this skill by the time we are in our twenties, and the most fundamental belief in the skill of self-consciousness is that the universe is an indivisible whole. It is known that giving priority in actions to eldering ourselves, our children, and our agreements to full maturity in the skill of self-consciousness is the only priority in the human skill of self-consciousness that is *simultaneously* best for each and all. It is without any experience of conflict between the two, between personal self-interest and the common good.

# 6
# Why the Elder Body and Congress Governance Model?

IT IS TIME FOR US TO MOVE UP THE LAYERS OF MATURITY of the ways we can cooperate together, from competition and compromise to agreement and love.

Let's make agreements and keep them. Let's also know we can at any time renegotiate any existing agreements into a different agreement.

Many of our best people shrink from running for political office in the geographic nations because they do not want to participate in a competitive process where winning rather than love is the priority.

Winning as the priority is the opposite of relating lovingly as the priority.

Giving priority to winning easily seduces us into activities that are not loving behaviors, such as marketing, trickery, lying, and stealing. Almost anything can be justified in our thinking when we give priority to winning.

*It is still living in the illusion that there are separate parts and a separate part is more important than participation in the maturation of us all.*

We are now ready to move into a governance process based on a more mature way of relating.

What is needed is the design of a process that has a high probability of having us consistently give priority to participation in the maturation of the universe. We want to give second priority to the making and keeping of agreements with each other.

*The purpose of the Elder Body is to institutionalize this.*

The Elder Body has two responsibilities and only two:

### *Two Responsibilities of the Elder Body*

1. To make sure all agreements made by the Community or Congress give priority to the maturation of the universe, and
2. To assist parents in the eldering of our children and each other in our

self-eldering into full maturity in the skill of self-consciousness as early in their/our lives as possible.

The contract between the Elder Body and the Communities or Congresses described in the Constitution is for the purpose of having there be a Body, the Elder Body, whose sole responsibility is to give priority to these two most important responsibilities of any human organization.

In the Communities and Associations, the Elder Body has the ultimate power. However, it delegates full responsibility for operations to the Congress while retaining the right to veto any decision made by it. A process is presented for monitoring the Congress. Whenever there is a concern or disagreement, the goal is for an agreement to be reached by the two bodies with the process facilitated by the Elder Body. If it deems necessary, the Elder Body has the ability to demand that new people be elected to the Community's or Congress's Board of Facilitators. However, it will try to never do this.

This puts a high responsibility on each Community to do a good job of choosing only those who have achieved full maturity in the skill of self-consciousness to be on their Elder Body. The Community chooses the first members. From that point forward, both the Elder Body and the Community must agree on any people appointed to the Elder Body. Those on the Elder Body then need to do a good job of keeping each other consistently operating at the highest layer of maturity in the skill of self-consciousness. Of course, when they need it, they can call on any others to assist them, particularly members of other Elder Bodies.

Secondly, there is nothing more important in the CGN than the eldering of all as early as possible in their lives into full maturity in the skill of self-consciousness.

*This is the only skill mastered by every child that can permanently bring an end to the minor and major conflicts on Earth.*

Imagine all the children on Earth being eldered to full maturity in the skill of self-consciousness by the time they are twenty years old. There would no longer be a need for armaments. Police would not need guns. Wars would only be in the history books. Courts could also be primarily in the history books replaced in most cases by the Clearing Process or mediation. Prisons would only be in the history books.

Businesses would voluntarily give priority to the common good and second priority to profit or anything else. Each would reach agreements with their competitors in each product area, as sports teams do, on the common good rules of play, for instance having the minimum wage be a livable wage in each production location. They would only secondly compete as ferociously as before but always within their freely chosen common good rules of play.

There would not be poverty. Every family would have the minimum necessary to live a healthy and happy life and the parents will be excited about playing whatever part they can play in the maturation of us all through a job in a common good company or organization.

People could still start and build companies or other organizations, but they would always choose to be common good organizations or there would not be public support for them. It would be a standard of which all would be aware and consistently honor. And, yes, then one of the highest priorities of our Earth village will be to occupy other planets.

Remember, there was a day when we thought the Earth was flat and electricity and democracy were a dream. Dreamers 2000 years ago knew this day would come. It has come. The above day will come also. Maturation is the fundamental process in nature.

The second priority of the Elder Body is to keep all of us on this self-eldering path. There are all kinds of educational and other programs they could create for this purpose.

The Board of Facilitators of the Community is responsible for its operations. Its members are chosen by the community including by the members of the Elder Body.

Each individual has the greatest power. At any time, he or she can leave the Community, remain a citizen of the CGN without being a member of a Community, join another Community, or leave the CGN completely. Each Community has the second greatest power. At any time, it or any of its citizens can abandon its Elder Body and Community Board of Facilitators and form another Common Good Community. The Elder Body has the third greatest power. And the Community Board of Facilitators has the fourth greatest power.

The responsibility of the Community's and Congress's Board of Facilitators is to identify where the community is ready to go, name it, reach agreement with the community members that their judgement is accurate, and then design programs in which usually but not always most will want to participate. There will be some good programs all support but in which only a few will choose to participate.

The Community Board of Facilitators does not have the power to tell the Community's citizens what to do. This is not a paternalistic system. It only has the power to *facilitate* the meeting of the needs and wants of the community.

*This is an organization based on agreements, not power. And it is based on giving priority to the maturation of the universe not winning.*

If the Board of Facilitators of the Communities or Congresses do not come up with a program the citizens like, the citizens will not participate. This is how the citizens have the greatest power and the Board of Facilitators of the Communities or Congresses the fourth most power.

*Their responsibility is to lead, not dictate, order, or demand.*

This is not easy for people to learn to do when they have only experienced hierarchy as primarily a power system instead of as primarily an efficiency system.

In 1983, some couples including my wife and I created a community that continues to this day. Its name became the Friends and Lovers Community. For me it was an experiment to see if we could discover how to re-village our lives in a modern context. It began as twenty couples and a single person, expanded to usually have as many as 60-70 adults and 30-40 children, and usually mainly met for two or three three-day holiday weekends equally distributed throughout the year: Memorial Day Weekend in May, Columbus Day Weekend in October, and Presidents Day Weekend in February. We also met as small groups or as a community many other times during the year.

On the three-day weekends, we would go to my wife's mother's horse riding camp for girls in central Connecticut and sleep in the cabins for the girls or in tents. On Friday nights, we would have a circle and "check-in." This is where we shared with each other the main adventures occurring in our lives. On Saturday morning, we would have people volunteer to do workshops or activities and schedule them throughout the weekend. Before dinner on Saturday, we would have a variety show, making sure to include the children and celebrate everyone's talents regardless of what level of skill, do skits, and just laugh a lot. On Saturday night, we would usually have an elaborate ritual in the woods. On Sunday mornings, we would do sweat lodges.

This is an ancient tradition particularly popular with Native Americans of heating up rocks, putting them in a pit in the ground inside a wickiup. It is bent saplings that have been used to create an igloo looking structure no higher than five feet above the ground that is covered with blankets so when the flap is closed there is no light inside. A hole is dug in the center where rocks are placed that have been heated in a large fire to where they glow red. The person leading the sweat guides those sitting in a circle around the glowing rocks into prayers and personal sharing of feelings and thoughts with the purpose being personal healing. At times, he or she sprinkles water on the hot rocks to create the equivalent of a steam bath experience. Afterwards we run and jump in the pond for the thrilling experience of our bodies going from being very hot to being quickly very cold. Then to our eyes, everything is shimmering. It is healing fun.

Sunday night we would have a dance. Musicians were always present and playing throughout. On Monday mornings, we would have a closing circle, bring all the children in and celebrate them, and share what was most fulfilling and wonderful about the weekend before going home.

When couples or any two people in our community would have a significant conflict, they could call for a Council. They would invite the people they judge best to facilitate if for them. It would be at someone's home. We developed different methods for facilitating them, from methods focused on reflective listening to methods very much like the Clearing Process presented in the Constitution.

We also created elaborate initiations for both boys and girls with the most popular one being for our young teenage boys. After the first one three of us did with a fourteen-year-old boy, we thought it was a disaster, we had no idea how to do it well, and promised ourselves we would never do that again until we learned much more on how to do it well. The boy barely talked the entire afternoon.

Yet when he returned from living with his father for a period of time, he asked to meet with us again. He treated us like we were very important elders in his life who deeply cared about him and more than advice he just wanted to bathe in our care for him and experience the safe place he felt with us to share his most intimate feelings in his relationship with his father and mother. We instantly realized that it wasn't so important what we had done that Saturday afternoon. What was most important to him was that our level of care for him was at a level that had us choose to do it. Years later, after college and working for some years, he returned to visit our community and broke down crying at how important and beautiful that experience had been for him.

Now, by the end of the day, we also share with each young teenager the layers of maturity of the skill of self-consciousness. We often guide the boy into an eye-to-eye experience of oneness in relationship with his father that is described in a book I wrote, *Eldering: What We Do Between Enlightenment and Death*. The relationship of the two of them changes from the paternalistic system of childhood to the equals-with-qualifications-relationship of teen-adult.

From that point forward the agreement is that decisions will be made by consensus with his parents. However, if consensus cannot be reached, by default his parents have the final say. On the other hand, very effort will be made to have the decisions be made by consensus agreement. This is seen by us as an honoring of and assisting him to master the teen layer of maturity. This also requires him to be continuously talking with his parents to make these agreements. The parents instantly realize this is important for their relationship with him as he moves through his teen years.

The women sometimes do a similar ritual with our young teenage girls, often around the time of her first menstruation.

Of course, at times in Friends and Lovers there have been Men's, Women's, and Couple's Groups. Also, music playing groups, party groups, and many other kinds of groups. There are rituals when a baby is about to be born and for many other occasions. The essence of each is heartfelt sharing with each other. Many in our community have become very good at creating effective and moving rituals.

The primary purpose of Friends and Lovers has been to re-village our lives in a modern context that feels full of joy and comfortable intimacy that radiates into deeply caring relationships with each other. On that score card, it has been a big success.

However, I have primarily described our Friends and Lovers Community to tell you the story of our effort to find a modern structure that is nurturing rather than dictatorial. From the beginning, primarily because we wanted to be sure we did not settle into a traditional power structure, our organizational structure has been a very loose one. There were people who loosely began to be seen as elders, leaders in the community. However, the only formal organizational structure was what was called the Dead End Gang, the group of people who hung out on the dock at the end of the weekends and figured out who were most appropriate to be the facilitators for the next weekend. Everything else was solely the result of self-initiative which, by the way, resulted in many self-initiated activities.

One time we decided to create a board of directors to have a more formal leadership structure for the community. *We were clear that it would be a facilitation group, not a dominant group.*

It immediately began to behave like all other boards of directors in American society. It began to be experienced as telling us what to do. Within months it was declared inoperative by the community. We went back to using the Dead End Gang Model and, now in our thirty-fourth year, we are still using it.

It is not easy to switch to the facilitation board of directors' model. The hierarchical power model is deep inside each of us. This is one of the main reasons it is valuable to have an Elder Body. Hopefully it is mature in these skills and can also be helpful when difficulties in this area emerge anywhere in the community.

The Community's and Congress's Board of Facilitators will have a Chair and perhaps other officers it chooses. It will facilitate the meeting of the needs and wants in the community and seek to be sure to do so in a way that is witnessed by all as giving priority to the maturation of the universe. They know the Elder Body has the ultimate power and is watching them from right in front of them. If they need help, they can call upon it or some of its members. If the two *ex officio members* from the Elder Body believe a decision is moving in a direction that is not giving priority to our maturation, they will ask for a meeting of the Community or Congress Board of Facilitators with the Elder Body's Board of Facilitators. In this way, the priority of all is on fashioning agreements on what is best for all, all humans and everything else as one whole, instead of a part of the universe winning and gaining power relative to the rest of it.

Finally, in each Community, each Elder Body Board of Facilitators elects two representatives to the Elder Body of the Local Association of Communities that constitutes its Elder Body. Each Community Board of Facilitators elects two of its members to the Congress of the Local Association of Communities that constitutes its Congress Body. Each of these Bodies elect two representatives to the next layer of Association. This continues until all the Communities are represented in an Association and no Association is larger than 100 people. This is to make sure the CGN can get as big as necessary to accommodate all Communities and all the people in each Body can get to know each other well. This will greatly enhance the possibility that wise decisions will be made of who is best chosen for each Body and next Association.

This also eliminates elections by millions of people who can easily be tricked by marketing skills, trickery, lies, fake news, and other forms of manipulation. It will also attract the most qualified people. It will be attractive to serve where the highest priority is the maturation of us all. Finally, it is also being done in a way that reflects the maturity of this effectively being its highest priority.

# 7
# Some of the Kinds of Projects That Could Be Launched by a Common Good Nation

Anything that the citizens of the CGN want that is not being done well or at all by the geographic nation can be launched by CGN. It will also take actions to help the geographic nations operate better.

As mentioned earlier, this means the geographic nations are going to love the emergence of CGN: it is the equivalent of a free research and development program. Anything it launches that works well at meeting a need or want of its citizens and others and gains widespread and strong support will be copied, if possible, or at least supported by the geographic nation.

*Many solutions to problems are best solved in the private for-profit or non-profit sector. In these cases, the geographic nations will find ways to provide support, such as tax breaks and other incentives.*

In this chapter, only a few of the many different kinds of groups and organizations that could be created by CGN will be presented to reveal the diversity of the kinds of organizations that can be created.

## Trusts for All Children

If we take on for a moment the assumption that the Earth now behaves much like one village and we are elders in the village, there are few things more important than ending poverty for all. The purpose of Trusts for All Children, Inc. (TAC) is to set something in motion in the private sector that we know will eventually accomplish this goal. Here is how it is currently designed to work. It is close to being able to be launched. The final legal work will be done soon and then all that will be needed is a $1 million loan to launch it: at a low interest rate the loan can be repaid over a seven-year period.

As it was described in the Constitution, TAC has two programs. One is to raise donations in the Common Good Fund. They are invested in common good companies. The annual profits are distributed to poor people around the world, in cash if necessary through responsible organizations. This way the donations will be solely used to invest in common good companies and it is their profits that will be ending poverty on Earth.

Warren Buffet and Bill and Melinda Gates have created an association of billionaires, now 115 members, who have all committed to donating 50% of their assets to charity before they die. The hope is that some of this capital will be donated into the Common Good Fund that will be solely committed to ending poverty on Earth.

The second one is a way for parents to create a trust fund for each of their children so their entire lives they do not have to worry about at least extreme poverty.

When a child is about to be born, the parents—or a religious community, non-profit, business, or town— invite at least ten family members and friends to commit to donate $10 a month by electronic transfer ($120 a year by each) for the first twenty years of the child's life. If mom and dad do it, both sets of grandparents do it, and there are two Godmothers and Godfathers who do it, that is ten people. There could be more and, of course, throughout the entire life of the child anyone can donate more to have the trust fund grow, particularly on birthdays, graduations, marriages, and other important events, including as distributions from wills.

If ten people contribute *and there are no other contributions the child's entire life,* at twenty years old the child's trust will have received $24,000. At eighteen-years old, the child will begin receiving a monthly distribution from the trust. It will continue until the child dies. If the stock market does what it has done for the last eighty-nine years, including 1929 (10.3% annual average), when elderly the child will be receiving a monthly distribution equal to a current average social security distribution. Of course, it will be more if there are contributions to the trust beyond the $24,000. All from a private sector program where geographic nation action cannot end it or change it. TAC could eventually provide this opportunity for all parents on Earth.

The capital will also grow without taxation. TAC will be using the Pooled Income Fund program of the US Internal Revenue Service (IRS). This will allow the capital to grow without taxation the entire time. Distributions to recipients are ordinary income for their tax responsibilities. This tax-exempt growth of capital is granted by the IRS in exchange for the balance upon the child's death remaining in TAC and being added to the Common Good Fund to end poverty on Earth.

Those who contribute to each child's trust know they are accomplishing two things. They are providing financial security to the child and upon his or her death they know the balance will solely be used to end poverty on Earth. When that is accomplished, the annual profits will help those receiving the least receive a little bit more.

Each contributor will contribute $11 a month instead of $10 and the extra dollar will cover the expenses for both the Common Good Fund and the Children's Trusts Program. *This way no expenses are deducted from the annual profits of the Common Good Fund distributed to poor families each year and all know that is the policy.*

Of course, many other programs can be created to reduce poverty. This is one that could raise much capital, have the profits of common good companies be the capital to end poverty, and will eventually end poverty on Earth.

## Common Good Fellowships

A program can be created where anyone at any age could create a fellowship to fund him or her doing a service to the community.

Using a 501(c )(3) tax-exempt charitable, educational, literary, and scientific organization, people could seek tax-deductible donations to cover the costs of them doing a project of their choice, much as Kickstarter, Indiegogo, and others do now. The difference is that those seeking a fellowship would describe the project they want to do that fits into one of the above categories and is a service to humanity. It could be volunteering to assist a classroom teacher, it could be volunteering with Doctors Without Borders, it could be working on a piece of art, it could be working on discovering cold fusion, or it could be writing a novel. It could be anything that would be an acceptable project by the IRS's rules within one of the above categories. Once approved the person could seek tax-deductible donations to fund his or her project, even on an on-going basis.

I assisted a psychotherapist friend to do this. She wanted to spend some of her time playing the harp for people when they are dying. For years now friends have supported her with donations from one annual mailing. It has allowed her to do this with a significant portion of her time.

## Common Good Capitalism

I have written a book on this: *Common Good Capitalism Is Inevitable.* It argues that the inevitable next layer of maturity of capitalism is common good capitalism.

This is where business owners give priority to the common good and second priority to profit or anything else. I believe it is inevitable because it is the only maturation that builds on individual freedom and free markets, two commitments we do not want to end.

Companies in a product market, like airlines, pharmacies, and home improvement, will come together like the teams in a sports league and reach agreement on the "common good rules of play." They will then continue to compete as ferociously as in the past. Like in sports leagues whether the National Basketball Association (NBA) or a local girls' soccer league, the difference is there are referees. The referees in these business leagues will be the financial auditors. They will report if and how a company is keeping these agreements.

If they agree, for instance, to have the minimum wage be the living wage in each location, they will all make the change on the same day. Thus, relative to each other it will not cost the companies a penny.

*This will have the multinationals and all companies become good guys.*

Nothing else will change. They can reach any agreements they choose. It will all be open to the public by posting the agreements and annual audits on the Internet. It will not be acceptable to give priority collectively to the owners, shareholders, and employees at the expense of the rest of us. And the public will be able to participate in the discussions of what would be wise additional common good agreements for our times.

This maturation of capitalism using the sports league model is inevitable because there is no other action that builds on individual freedom and free markets, the teen layer of human maturity. Finally, the rapid consolidation of companies toward becoming nationally, regionally, or globally duopoly monopolies in product markets so they can more easily match each other's fundamental price increases will eventually bring this about in one of the two following ways or as a combination of both. Some CEOs and boards will realize it will be wise to be first in the marketplace to do this. That will begin a cascade of all companies doing it. Or when the public becomes aware of this rapid growth toward duopoly monopolies they demand our maturation into common good capitalism.

In the USA, only four airlines, Delta, American, United, and Southwest, control 80% of airline seats. CVS and Walgreens control 90% of pharmacies. Home Depot and Lowe's, UPS-FedEx, Pepsi-Coca Cola, Boeing-Air- bus and many more product companies control a high percentage of their markets. This makes it easy to match each other's fundamental price increases which is monopoly behavior through a back door. The ease of doing this when the number of companies in a market is small is one of the main reasons for the high level of merger and acquisition activity today. Thus, it is only a matter of time before there is a movement toward common good capitalism. CGN can take the lead here.

## Some Projects That Could Be Launched To Improve Geographic Operations

### *Majority Supported Platform*

When deciding to vote, a way to escape the extensive manipulation of our thinking by marketing people, fake news, and trickery is to put together a platform only of positions where polls show 60% of Americans support them. Then near elections this group can let voters know the candidates to vote for who are genuinely committed to supporting the positions of the platform.

Here is how this could be done in every state in the US. Let's use Vermont as an example.

There are 626,000 people in Vermont. The largest turnout in the last three presidential elections was 318,236. If we took a platform such as the one above to voters and got each person to commit to vote for the candidates who commit to supporting it, to get them elected it would be necessary to have 160,000 people in Vermont vote for them. If when they committed to it each one was given a number such as 32, 157, 5,039, and 134,301, when they all knew that 160,000 or more had committed to that platform they would know that if they went to the polls and voted they would succeed in electing the candidates who support it.

*This would have them highly motivated to vote and vote that way: they would want to maintain solidarity with the other 160,000 plus voters to achieve it.*

The recruitment could happen door to door, via the Internet, at every kind of meeting in the state, and anywhere people could be contacted and asked to sign on to it. Each would receive their number via the Internet so each would have their unique number.

This would not be a Democratic or Republican Party activity. This would be the action of an independent organization, the Majority Supported Platform, Inc., that seeks to identify where a majority of Americans agree and making sure they get candidates elected that *at least* support the positions supported by a majority of Americans.

It would also be made clear that not all issues will be spoken to on the platform. It would intentionally be limited to those positions where polls show there is at least a 60% support. Positions on issues that do not have this level of support will not be on the platform. That way the purpose of this program is clear: to elect candidates who support positions supported by 60% of the voters.

We know a significant majority of voters support a sustainable environment. We know they support rapid conversion to renewable energy. We know they support making it easy for all people to vote. We know they support equal rights for women. We know they support providing leadership to make the world a better place for all, not just Americans. We know they support military alliances that sustain peace. We know they support diplomacy and avoiding wars. We know they support an economy where the minimum wage is a livable wage. We know they support entrepreneurship and the ability for people to make significant profits as a result, but they also support employees receiving wages that allows for the growth rather than shrinking of the Middle Class.

True democracy is when the people elected genuinely support the important positions of a significant majority of the people of the nation. A Majority Supported Platform program in every state could accomplish it.

## *People's Committees: A Parallel Political System With No Legal Power, But the Greatest Political Power*

I was stunned to read in a Nicholas Kristof's column in the *New York Times* that a research group discovered that during the three months of the 2016 US Presidential campaign less than five hours was used to discuss issues by all the television programs covering it combined. In other words, more than 95% percent of the time was used to talk about the horserace.

The priority of the television stations is to hold people's attention to watch the commercials. Is the media still the Fourth Estate, primarily responsible for making sure all leaders are acting for the common good? I know all media are not the same. So for each media source I will let you decide your answer to this question

*It is time for us to create in each local area in the geographic nations a parallel political system. It is focused on guiding communities in discussions over time and without a deadline toward a significant majority agreeing on a position on each important issue.*

Here is how I think People's Committees (PCs) could come into existence anywhere. This could also be one of the projects to support the geographic nations by local CGN Communities or Congresses.

Any group of people in any community could create one. They would probably establish themselves as a non-profit corporation and recruit a number of respected leaders in the community to be on the board of directors. They would raise a small amount of capital to get started.

They would then invite every major church, the downtown business association, the manufacturer's association, the women's association, the major non-governmental organizations, the farmers' association, and the major non-profit and for-profit corporations to each elect their senior most respected statesperson to represent them on the PC. Criteria for which organizations would be invited would be created with an interest in having representatives from all walks of life in the community. The purpose of the board of directors and staff would be to facilitate the discussions and keep the community informed of the meetings and decisions of the PC.

*Anyone involved in electoral politics would not be able to participate. The purpose of this organization is going in the exact opposite direction of electoral politics. Whereas they are participating in competitive activity to win elections, the members of the PC are seeking to cooperate over time in a genuine search for truth for the purpose of coming to a 70% agreement on each issue.*

There is skillful facilitation and the members sit in circles. To reduce the numbers, members could form into groups, perhaps based on interest and product areas, and appropriately rotate members of the PC participating into the inner circle. The proceedings could be watched by an audience, both in person and via television and cellphones.

Any issue that is up front and important to the community could be brought up for discussion, for instance making it easy for people to vote, a woman's right to an abortion, environment policies, or many motorcyclists coming to town on Friday night. The PC would then schedule the evening for a discussion by members, or the people they bring forward.

If the vote at the end of the first evening of discussion is less than 70% but more than 40%, an evening is scheduled for the discussion to continue. It could be next week, next month, or the same month the following year. The latter would provide time for people to prepare their arguments. There would be a short time to the next meeting if it is a pressing issue.

The goal is to have a format where significant issues can be discussed in a mutually respectful way, without a deadline, and to eventually form an agreement on each issue that 70% of the PC members support.

However, that is not what is most important. What is most important is that there is a place for such discussions and the entire community can both participate and witness the direction in which the consistently growing percentage is moving.

*The result will eventually be that, although it will have no legal power, it will in fact be the most powerful political body in the community.*

Usually no candidate could easily get elected who does not support the positions supported by more than 70% of the members of the PC or where the vote, perhaps 52% or 63%, reveals the direction of the community.

Finally, the PC can also be the place where steam can be blown off so people can get back down to civil behavior with each other. For instance, if there is outrage throughout the community because of the treatment of a Native-American coach at the high school, the PC can call an immediate meeting solely for the purpose of assisting people to discover the facts as best as possible and to share their thoughts and feelings about the processes and policies at the high school.

*The PC would be a parallel political system solely focused on facilitating a caring process for discussions toward agreements on important issues. It would happen face-to-face and without a deadline. This can allow the space necessary for people to find ways to move together based on a genuine search for truth for our time.*

It can be imagined that PCs could eventually spread around the world and into every community in every nation. Little by little conventional governments will come to deeply appreciate the stability, civility, and caring nature of the PCs and not only welcome them into their community but actively champion their establishment. Their financial costs can initially be covered by contributions from foundations and members of the community and eventually they could be funded with tax dollars.

It could also begin to affect the way the geographic nations conduct their affairs.

# Conclusion

ALLOW ME TO CONCLUDE THIS BOOK WITH THE STORY OF Mahatma Gandhi's effort to create a more mature democracy in India. As you probably know, Gandhi was the person who led India to freedom from England in the 1930s and 1940s. He has also been the inspiration for non-violent movements around the world, including those led by Martin Luther King, Jr. in the USA in the 1950s and 1960s.

In my judgment, both the creation of the People's Committees described in the last chapter and the CGN are descendants of his thinking. His work creating People's Committees ended with his assassination. Decades later one of his followers picked up the idea and grew it into a huge success throughout India. However, to his great regret, when he allowed it to be used to support an electoral campaign it dissolved.

I now believe there are two ways we can continue building Gandhi's dream and the dreams of many: the creation of the CGN and People's Committees in the geographic nations. They are both ways of having our existing majoritarian democracies work better.

Here is the story of Gandhi's effort and how it eventually spread throughout India.

The last two years of his life he basically renounced all that he had done before and returned to the villages to create a more mature democracy. Some people thought Gandhi was losing his mind. He was the most powerful man in India even already having the title of the "Father of India." Yet he left the halls of power and returned to the villages to start something brand new. Gandhi's judgment on himself was that he had made a large mistake in creating the Congress I Party as a political party in a competing political party system.

Gandhi understood the universe to be an indivisible whole where by nature all the parts had the purest of primary intentions, that is, to cooperate with one another for the good of the one whole.

Therefore, to build a political system based on competition rather than cooperation was to consistently polarize people into competing camps.

That was the opposite of the kind of community and society Gandhi wanted to create. He believed this was going in the opposite direction of nature and it would, therefore, consistently result in misery for many.

Further, he believed that he had perpetuated this immature approach by creating the Congress I Party as a competing political party in such a system. He judged that to some degree this mistake made him personally responsible for the separation of India into India and Pakistan. He decided that, with what energy he had left in him before he died, he needed to successfully demonstrate a more mature form of democracy.

In Gandhi's thinking, a majoritarian democracy was not really as much a democracy as it was the last form of dictatorship before real democracy - the dictatorship of the majority over the minority. Rather than the leadership of the opposing groups sitting down and talking to one another, they organized their armies of followers and fought each other through ballots and the media…and seldom spoke to each other. It perpetuated war games rather than love games. Winning rather than losing became most important instead of the discovery of more mature truths together.

So, he returned to the villages and began to create what he called "Peoples Committees (PC)." It was based on the ancient *panchayat* tribal systems of India. The way it functioned was as follows.

The main affinity groups in the village were identified. In today's small towns and as described in the last chapter, it might be every major church, the downtown business association, the manufacturer's association, the women's association, the major non-governmental organizations, the farmers' association, and the major non-profit and for-profit corporations. Each group would be invited to elect their senior, most mature person, to serve on the PC. The only people who could not serve on the PC were those directly involved with electoral politics.

They were going in the opposite direction.

They were organizing against an opposition. The PC was based on finding consensus. The PC was looking to find common ground and to co-create greater understanding. While accepting all the differences that existed, it invited these elders in the community to search to identify as many agreements as they could find to peel off from their disagreements so the primary focus would be on the donut of agreements that would became larger and larger relative to the differences, the crumbs, still in the middle of the donut. The PC was seeking to find agreement, hopefully with 100% voting for the agreement but, if not, be able to observe the percentages going higher or lower each time the proposed, or amended, agreement was again discussed. The PC would be open for anyone to attend. In fact, the entire village was encouraged to sit in a circle around the PC circle. In today's world, this possibility could be enhanced with the use of television, smartphones, radio, and computers.

Gandhi's belief was that since this was a more mature way for people to relate, the result would be that the elected officials would never be able to go against the consensus decisions, or near consensus decisions, of the village sitting with the "village elders."

He believed the result would be that people would slowly shift their priorities and give greater priority to the PC than to the competing political party governance system.

In this innocent and non-confrontational way, the PC would become primary; the competitive process would become secondary; and, hopefully and eventually, the official competitive process would be reorganized to be more like the People's Committee process. The PC was Gandhi's non-violent strategy to bring about this maturation of democracy.

Gandhi had only begun to create these People's Committees when he was assassinated.

There was a man named Jayprakash Narayan (JP) who was head of the Socialist Party in India during the time in the late 1940s that Gandhi began to work on this. He became disillusioned with the perspective of the socialists and communists, resigned, and fully left the organization.

He went to the ashram of Vinoba Bhave, one of Gandhi's followers, where he meditated on these things from the late 1940s until the mid-1960s. At that point, he came across an account of what Gandhi was trying to do the last couple years of his life and realized that Gandhi had discovered how to create a more mature form of democracy and was in the process of creating it when he was assassinated.

JP left the ashram and began traveling around India telling this story to students, followers of Gandhi, and others. He then organized them to go into the villages to set up People's Committees. They did this throughout India with rapid and substantial success.

In 1975, Indira Gandhi, the Prime Minister, decided to let her opposition out of jail and call a national election for about six weeks away. Her belief was that none of her opposition fragmented into many small parties would be able to unite and organize against her in that short period of time. She would end up with such an overwhelming victory that she would have a large mandate to govern.

None of the many smaller parties were as widespread and politically strong as the PCs. Many within the PC movement argued that to save India JP needed to support converting the PCs into a political party to overthrow Indira Gandhi. JP said no. He explained that the entire purpose of creating the People's Committees was to create a more mature democratic process then the current competitive political party system. He had to be true to Mahatma Gandhi's dream. It was his sacred responsibility.

The reason so many People's Committees had been created so rapidly was because people liked them. They preferred them to the other political system. He believed abandoning them would be an end to the mission of creating a more mature democratic process.

However, JP quickly realized that he was going to lose this argument. He then came up with a strategy that would allow the PCs to throw in their support only for the following six weeks to defeat Indira Gandhi's control of Parliament. Then the PCs would return to their normal role in the villages.

JP called representatives from the smaller political parties to his bedside. He was often on a dialysis machine and thought to be dying. JP pointed out that he had tried in 1974 to persuade Indira Gandhi to fight corruption and venality in public life. But she refused to deal with him. JP agreed that the priority was that she had to be defeated and that the only way to defeat her was for all the smaller parties to unite and put up only one candidate against the candidate from Indira Gandhi's party, the Congress I Party that Mahatma Gandhi had created. He would then support the PCs supporting the election of those candidates but only until the election.

They agreed to do it and the Janata Party, a coalition of all the smaller parties with the support of the PCs, came into existence. He also agreed that until the end of the election he would turn his attention to the majoritarian political process and work in collaboration with all the smaller parties to defeat Indira Gandhi.

In six weeks, their new coalition party, the Janata Party, agreed on candidates and had enough credibility and widespread support that they defeated Indira Gandhi. JP became known as the Second Father of India. He handpicked Moraji Daisai to be the Prime Minister.

Sadly, however, all in the People's Committees became an enthusiastic part of the now ruling Janata Party and the People's Committees disappeared. Gandhi's and JP's dream of a more mature form of democracy came to an end a second time.

In 1979 I was in India. I was a consultant to the grandson of one of the ruling families of India. He had a successful business in the USA and wanted to re-organize it into a trusteeship business.

"Trusteeship" was Mahatma Gandhi's word for his theory of economics. He believed that, since the universe is an indivisible whole, we are all trustees of our wealth and skills and are to primarily manage them for the good of all and only secondly take what we needed and no more. We are not primarily owners who use all we can get our hands on for our own self-interests. At the same time, what we kept for ourselves had to be a free decision, not imposed by any outside force such as a government. This decision is part of our maturation process. That is more important.

The Indian-American businessman hired me to assist him to convert his business into a trusteeship business. He, fourteen of his top employees, and I journeyed to India to study trusteeship. We were able to have a meeting with JP because the man who hired me was the man who had provided JP the funds to buy the dialysis machine.

At this time, JP was the spiritual as well as the political leader of India. A few days before we met with him, there had actually been fistfights in the Lok Sabat (the Parliament) over the issue of allowing the slaughter of cows so people could eat the meat. The Hindu religion, as you may know, is against the slaughter of cows for food. The next day the front page of the *India Times* reported that JP believed it was too early in the changes that were occurring to take on this issue and that it should be tabled for a later time. The following day the Lok Sabat voted unanimously to table the question. This was the kind of power JP had in India at the time. He was the spiritual leader, the Second Father of India.

When we met with him, we had half an hour to ask him questions. Then he would have a short press conference after which we learned he was scheduled to have another dialysis treatment. As the main spokesperson for the group, I asked him questions about trusteeship for the entire half hour. I knew what he would probably give as answers to all the questions. I was focusing on using the time to establish a very deep, quality relationship with him. I really only had one question I wanted to ask him.

At the end of the time I said that I had one last question for him and it would be OK if he chose to not answer it. I would understand.

"Go right ahead," he responded.

Not knowing at the time that he had not intended for the People's Committees to become part of the Janata Party, I said, "If you had to do it over again, would you have converted the People's Committees into the Janata Party?" The public officials and news media in the back of the room, who had been quietly jabbering away, suddenly shushed each other into silence. I was fully aware that I was asking the question that was not to be asked. I also knew I was an American visitor and could get away with it. After learning all I had learned up to that point, especially since arriving in India, I was very curious how he would answer it.

JP assumed my question was accurate, which was telling in itself, and gave me the politically correct answer. "It was a difficult time in the history of India. We had to take a decision. We looked at all sides of the issue and concluded that it was best for India at the time for us to turn our attention to the conventional political process."

Then he looked me straight in the eyes steadily without blinking and a bit slowly said, "Does my intelligent American friend have any other questions for me?" He gave a certain kind of emphasis on the word "intelligent" as he starred deep into my eyes such that I knew clearly what he was saying to me. Without blinking either, I looked straight back into his eyes and said a bit slowly, "Thank you so very, very much."

With his eyes, he had clearly communicated to me that it had been a mistake to turn his attention to the conventional political process. Only upon research into discovering the whole story I am now telling you did I discover that his plan was to have the PCs continue after the election. He was now stuck making the best of the situation as the spiritual leader of the nation's majoritarian democracy.

In that moment, I could feel his sadness. I now know it was because he believed he had let Mahatma Gandhi and humanity down. Like Gandhi, he had come to see the importance of creating a building-toward-consensus-over-time democracy based on the assumption of oneness instead of separateness. He had given into the pressure of a moment and let it fall into disarray and become seduced into the conventional political process. There was a quality in his eyes of an older man speaking in code to a younger man from a foreign land who saw the truth of his situation.

With his eyes, he was saying, "If you see what happened with both Gandhi's and my effort, you have a responsibility to respond to that truth, step forward, and pick up where we left off." At that time, I was in my mid-thirties, not fully aware of the source of the sadness in his eyes, and even if I had been I would not have been equal to that challenge.

Six months later, JP died. On his deathbed, he told his secretary to report that it had been a mistake to turn his attention from the PCs and to electoral politics.

The Janata Party ended up being attacked by its enemies to the point, as with all parties in competing political systems, people did not know what was true or false. So, it became seen as just another corrupt political party. It lost the next election, the former smaller parties broke from it, and it soon disappeared from existence. It was almost as if JP had anticipated this would be the ultimate result once the Second Father of India was gone. Yet the PC movement had died a second time.

In my judgment, picking up the process of maturing democracy where Gandhi and JP left off requires the creation of two organizations: CGN and People's Committees.

CGN is for those who know the universe is an indivisible whole, self-consciousness is a skill, and we can master it by the end of our teen years. It is also transnational and, while the people are fully committed citizens of both, has the potential to be given a higher priority than their geographic nations. This could help reduce the possibility of conflict between and among the geographic nations. It can also model for the geographic nations a more mature form of democracy.

*In addition, the creation of People's Committees can be one of the projects of CGN in support of a more mature democratic process within the geographic nations.*

This consensus-building-over-time democratic process would be used by both. Communities and Congresses can create People's Committee Programs within CGN. It could also take the lead to create them in every town and city section of the geographic nations. Both would build toward a wider and wider agreement on issues based on a more and more mature understanding of truth.

The primary focus would be on the "donut of agreement" getting thicker and thicker, and the differences still inside the donut hole, like crumbs, getting smaller and smaller. People would now be talking with each other for the purpose of affirming that their priority is the common ground and respect each other for always seeking to know what is true and fashion it into agreements and programs appropriate for each of our particular communities.

As mentioned earlier, in the current competing political climate in democratic nations the right wing religious leader, the left-wing progressive, the feminist leader, the neo-capitalist, the Marxist, and the minority leader seldom talk to one another. They organize armies and fight each other through the media and ballot boxes. This is a very unhealthy, immature, polarizing, and a slow change way for social maturation to occur. It can also result in a minority getting control of government and taking it in an extremely immature direction.

In the PC system, these leaders are sitting in a circle and talking to one another eyes-to-eyes with the entire community watching. They are seeking to find where they can agree on things and how they can accept and adjust to the places where they disagree. They also are committed to continuing the conversation for the purpose of sorting through the disagreements to as much agreement as they can find. Most important, the focus is on finding a more mature understanding of truth together in the use of the skill of self-consciousness, not on winning in a game of right and wrong or imposing their super belief upon others. They are comfortably moving into a deeper understanding and trust of each other, not creating thicker walls between each other.

And the entire town, state, geographic nation, and planet is free to watch this process, and, of course, each person can participate at times as well. This applies pressure to be truthful and to focus on nothing other than finding deeper, wiser, and self-evident truths together.

*This is a maturing process rather than a fighting process.*

By staying in the conversation with one another, and the community insisting on openness and honesty in the search for truths that can be affirmed as true in direct experience and scientific research, more and more truth is uncovered and agreed upon. Once a truth can be seen, sooner or later there is no ability to act like it has not been seen.

*As stated in the* Introduction, *the wonderful thing about truth is that once we know it in direct experience we can't ever fool ourselves into thinking we do not know it.*

There are people on the planet who still think the Earth is flat. Given what we now know, within a reasonable period of time we all know that in a caring conversation these people would come to agree the Earth is round because it is round. It could be the same with an agreement, for instance, that all in geographic nations should have easy access to voting. There could be agreement on many issues like this where all would agree in eyes-to-eyes with each other rather than escaping contact with each other and giving priority to winning in a fight for power to force decisions on others.

Gandhi believed that when people sit in a circle and are committed to being open and honest in a genuine search for truth, when a person spoke something that resonated as true inside each of us it would be very difficult for those witnessing it to hold to their previous position and avoid honoring it. There would be smiles, joy, exaltation, and embracing rather than judgment and the throwing up of fingers indicating "we are number one!" In this very personal way, little by little a consensus on issues could be found.

CGN allows those who share its worldview to unite into a local and transnational organization. As we know, not all in any geographically area share this worldview. It is essential, therefore, that those of us who do share it unite in an organization that allows us to enjoy living together according to it and getting better at it.

This is why CGN is necessary. What happened to the People's Committees in India can happen to them if again launched in any geographic nation and probably will in some places. There emergence in the middle of a very polarized majoritarian democratic system will have many challenges. Therefore, we need to create both CGN so we can immediately begin living the way we want to live with each other and PCs in our geographic nations to assist them in a non-confrontational and loving way toward their maturation into a more mature democracy.

Those of us who already share a worldview will have an easier time reaching agreements on issues discussed in the PCs created within CGN. And CGN is the organization that will have the greatest ability to launch and sustain the PCs in the geographic nations.

Within CGN, PCs can be created by any Community or Association Congress. Representatives of all the Communities could elect their most mature statesperson to the CGNPC.

In summary, it is time we pick up from where Gandhi and JP left off. It is time for us to create a nation by agreement based on the more mature worldview that the universe is an indivisible whole, self-consciousness is a skill, and we can master it by the end of our teen years. Secondly, one of its services to the currently dominant geographic nations can be to create within them People's Committees to assist them in their maturation process.

The launching of these two organizations will be the maturation of democracy from majoritarian democracies and toward consensus-building-over-time democracies. They both use a mutually respectful and cooperative process in a genuine search for truth.

Truth can always be found. It is always there to be seen and never changes.

# The Rose on the Back Cover

The rose on the cover is what my father, Hienie Mollner, would draw beneath his name each time he signed a note or card with a gift. In Mollner's Meat Market, he would also add it beneath his hand-written magic marker signs on butcher paper for the particular sausage, such as jaternices, he wanted to make sure he sold that day. He would misspell it on purpose. He would then post it in a prominent place on the wall behind his butcher block. When a customer would point the misspelling out to him, he would act like he couldn't believe he had done that. He would then say, "Hey! Would you like some jaternices?" They would usually respond, "Sure Hienie, give me a couple jaternices."

When anyone asked him what the rose meant he would say, "That rose is always watching to be sure we are each following our conscience."

The three leaves represented the Father, Son, and Holy Spirit in his Catholic tradition. For me they represent the three dimensions of the skill of self-consciousness: recognition of differences, the mutual illusion tool of a human language that allows us to become self-conscious, and the oneness of nature. For all we know, since nothing was written down for over 60 years, these may have been the original generic meaning of the Son (recognition of differences), and the Holy Spirit (the mutual illusion tool of human language that allows us to self-consciously participate in the maturation of the universe), and the Father (the oneness of nature): the three dimensions of the skill of self-consciousness.

# About the Author

Terry Mollner, in the 1970s, was one of the earliest pioneers of socially responsible and community investing. With Robert Swann, he was a founder a founder of the Institute for Community Economics (ICE). Over eighteen months of monthly meetings, he guided fifteen leaders from around the country in the writing of one of the first set of social screens for investing. With Wayne Silby, one of those leaders, those screens were used to establish the Calvert Family of Socially Responsible Mutual Funds (www.calvert.com), the first family to such funds. Dr. Mollner served on its board from its founding in 1982 to 2016. Today it is one of the largest with $12 billion under management.

The team at ICE was also the creators of one of the first "community development financial institutes (CDFIs)." It made loans to low income housing projects, social and cooperative enterprises in low income communities, and microloan programs (small uncollateralized business loans). Today similar funds exist in communities throughout the US and are supported by annual funding from the US Government. This led to Dr. Mollner taking the lead to create the Calvert Foundation (www.calvertfoundation.org) to raise capital from investors to fund this industry. It has raised and loaned over $1.5 billion to reduce poverty around the world and is one of the largest contributors of capital to the growth to this movement.

Dr. Mollner continues to serve on the board of the Calvert Foundation and is now on the Calvert Advisory Board of the Funds that works to be sure high standards are sustained as socially responsible investment is becoming mainstream investing.

In 2000, he stepped up to assist Ben & Jerry's (www.benjerry.com) in its need to be bought by a multinational to deal with its distribution requirements as it was becoming a global brand. As part of its purchase by Unilever, he and the board arranged for a contract that allowed Ben & Jerry's to both continue to operate as an independent company and have a contract that obligated Unilever to allow it to continue forever to spend the same percentage of its annual budget on social activism as of the year it was bought. Ben & Jerry's is the only socially responsible company from the last half of the 20th century bought by a multinational to sign such a contract. Terry has been on its board since its purchase in 2000.

Dr. Mollner is also the founder and chair of Stakeholders Capital (www.stakeholderscapital.com), a socially responsible asset management firm with offices in Massachusetts and California. Since 1973 he has been the founder and executive director of Trusteeship Institute (www.commongoodmovement.com). Its current projects are the creation of Trusts for All Children, Inc. (www.trustsforallchildren.org), a membership program to create $24,000 starter trusts for the children of members with an equal amount of its earnings creating trusts for poor children around the world and building a Common Good Capitalism Movement. Another TI project is the Haiti Orphanage Sponsorship Trust (HOST) (www.crowdrise.com/haitianorphanage). It consistently funds an orphanage in Haiti with thirty-five children. He is also the author of *The Love Skill: We Are Each Mastering the 7 Layers of Human Maturity, Common Good Capitalism is Inevitable, Eldering: What We Do Between Enlightenment and Death,* and two books and many articles on the Mondragon Cooperatives in the Basque Region of northern Spain.

As part of his experiments to learn more about re-villaging our lives in a modern context, he is one of the founders of three intentional communities of friends that continue to exist: Spanish House, Hearthstone Village, and Friends and Lovers Community. He is also the creator of the Love Skill Weekend, a weekend where people work on mastering the skills of the highest layers of maturity of the human skill of self-consciousness (www.theloveskill.org).

Additional information can be found about CGN at –
www.commongoodnation.org.

Made in the USA
Middletown, DE
13 November 2021

51808216R10057